TEAMSTERS, PACKERS & BULLWHACKERS

True Tales of the Old West

by

Charles L. Convis

Watercolor Cover by Mary Anne Convis

PIONEER PRESS, CARSON CITY, NEVADA

Library of Congress Catalog Card Number: 96-68502

ISBN 1-892156-14-8

Printed by
KNI, Incorporated
Anaheim, California

CONTENTS

ILLUSTRATIONS

A GOOD AND HONEST MAN

William Lewis Manly was brought up in the Green Mountains of Vermont to treat people fairly and keep his word. He helped his family earn what little cash money they needed by making shingles, which sold ten for a penny.

Manly learned to treat animals kindly. In 1830, when he was nine, he drove a light wagon to Michigan Territory, where his family settled on two hundred acres about sixty miles west of Detroit.

When he was nineteen, Manly had three months of schooling, getting as far as the Rule of Three in his arithmetic book. With three younger brothers wanting to share the family land, he decided to go west and seek his fortune. With seven dollars in his pocket — four of which he had saved and three which tapped his father out — he traveled in a home-made boat down the Grand River, bought passage across Lake Michigan, and worked at whatever he could find in Wisconsin Territory.

"You must be a good boy, honest and law-abiding," his parents had said. "Remember our advice, and honor us for we have striven that you will become a good and honest man."

In 1849, when he heard of the gold discovery, Manly decided to go further west. He stored clothing, his main rifle, and other possessions with Asahel Bennett, a man with whom he had boarded one winter. Then he went to the Winnebago country to buy an Indian horse. Upon returning he learned that Bennett had left for California, taking Manly's outfit with him.

Manly rode to the Missouri River where he hired on as an ox-driver with Charles Dallas, captain of a five-wagon train from Iowa. Manly's wagon was pulled by a team of oxen and a team of cows. He had trouble at first, but when the animals learned that he was kind, they drove well.

John Haney Rogers, a butcher from Tennessee, was also a teamster for Dallas. Manly was small, about 5 feet 7 inches, but Rogers was 6 feet 2, and over two hundred pounds. Both, however, had quiet, gentle eyes and a kind demeanor. Rogers, about three years younger than Manly, drove a horse-drawn wagon.

When the wagon train was camped near Fort Kearney, a strange horse entered their herd. The next morning two soldiers rode up to inquire about the lost horse. Manly's New England ideas of honesty were shattered when Dallas denied knowing anything. When the train passed the fort a few hours later, Dallas concealed the army horse from the officers' view.

Traveling up the Sweetwater River in present Wyoming, the emigrants saw snow on the mountains. Dallas said it was too late to reach California before winter, so he would lay off his hired men when they reached Salt

Lake City. The men were upset about wintering with Mormons.

At the first west-flowing stream after crossing South Pass — the Big Sandy, a tributary of the Green — the hired teamsters saw an old, twelve-foot ferry boat half buried in a sand bar. They dug it out and decided to travel to the Pacific Ocean in it. Manly traded his Indian horse to Dallas for supplies, and the men set out by water to complete their journey to the goldfields.

Manly was elected captain, perhaps because he had once sailed from Michigan to Wisconsin. While passing through a deep canyon near Brown's Hole, they lost their boat on the rocks. The teamsters then made two fifteen-foot-long canoes out of pine trees, lashed them together for stability, and sailed on. But the canoes were too short for their load, so they made a thirty-foot canoe from a taller pine tree, again elected Manly captain of the little flotilla, and continued their journey.

In one reach of treacherous water they lost one canoe, four of their six guns, and almost lost one man. When they reached a camp of Chief Walkara of the Utes, the chief convinced them they could never reach the Pacific alive, so they walked to the valley south of Salt Lake City. There Manly was surprised to find Bennett and his family, waiting in a train to travel down the Old Spanish Trail to Southern California. He and Rogers joined that train to drive wagons.

When the train reached southwestern Utah, about twenty-seven wagons turned west into land never before crossed on wheels, the emigrants hoping to find a short cut to the goldfields. Of the six teamsters who had been hired by Dallas, only Manly and Rogers were with this group.

Most of the wagons traveled as fast as possible, their owners feeling no responsibility to the families with children. The four wagons belonging to the Asahel and Sarah Bennett and the John and Abigail Arcan families lagged behind. Manly felt that "Bennett was my friend and had been faithful to me and my property when he knew not where I was." He decided to stay with the Bennetts, although he no longer had a team to drive.

So Manly climbed mountains along the way to pick out the best route. Often he stayed out all night, and many times traveled alone for two or three days with only his canteen and gun. He was an excellent shot and had been a professional hunter, selling game to others. But after a few weeks he had seen only one rabbit, which he killed. By that time the oxen, fat when they left Salt Lake, were gaunt, barely able to drag the wagons.

Shortly after Christmas Manly killed a goose, the only bird he had seen. That and a few dead oxen, whose stringy flesh was hard to chew and swallow, was all the meat they had.

After crossing the Amargosa Valley in present Nevada and the Funeral Mountains of California, the emigrants descended into Death Valley, where Manly and Rogers scouted to find a way out.

The four teamsters hired to drive the Bennett-Arcan wagons abandoned the group and struck out on foot to find their own escape. Then Bennett and Arcan asked Manly and Rogers to go on alone and see if they could find a settlement and bring back food before anyone starved. The two teamsters agreed and climbed into the Panamint Mountains, hoping they would survive for the fifteen days it was assumed the rescue journey would take.

After three days they passed the body of a man from one of the parties traveling ahead, and they met up with others in those parties. The next day they met the four teamsters who had abandoned their party. The four begged for food which Manly and Rogers shared with them. All they had was ox meat, stripped, cooked, and dried when the animals perished. Everything better had been left behind for the women and children.

On the ninth day they shot a crow and a small hawk, their first fresh meat. That evening they shot a quail and hoped they were nearing civilization. Two days later they saw a herd of cattle grazing over "broad areas of luxuriant grass." Manly wrote: "They were of all colors, shades and sizes. Some were calmly lying down in happy rumination, others rapidly cropping the sweet grass, while the gay calves worked off their superfluous life and spirit in vigorous exercise or drew rich nourishment in the abundant mother's milk. All seemed happy and content, and such a scene of abundance and rich plenty and comfort bursting thus upon our eyes which for months had seen only the desolation and sadness of the desert, was like getting a glimpse of Paradise, and tears of joy ran down our faces."

Manly shot a yearling steer, and they feasted that evening and made new moccasins from the green hide. The next day they met a man who invited him to stay at his house while he arranged for supplies in Los Angeles, thirty miles away.

That evening they enjoyed corn meal and their first vegetable food for weeks. They ate too much, and severe stomach pains kept them awake most of the night.

The next night they reached the San Fernando Mission and the following day — their fourteenth — they returned to the house where they had eaten the corn meal. They had many offers of assistance, but all required considerable delay. Manly and Rogers worried that the Bennett-Arcan party would give up waiting and try to escape on their own. They knew that would be fatal for most of the women and children.

So the two young teamsters, with no family connections to the starving emigrants, having come close to death themselves in their own escape, and without a thought of just going on to the goldfields, did everything they could to hurry back and help the people they had traveled with. Using a mill at the house, they ground wheat into flour, prepared some dried meat, and obtained a sack of wheat and a sack of beans. They bought two horses, pack saddles and ropes, loaded their supplies, and set off for Death Valley.

On the first night of their return trip they overtook a wagon party and spent their last money buying a little one-eyed mule and another horse. Now they could each ride and lead a pack animal. The wagon party also gave them supper, breakfast, and twenty-five pounds of flour.

After two more days their animals were traveling so slowly they divided the loads among the four and walked themselves.

The next day one of the horses died; they divided its load among the others and continued. That night they cached their flour to make the loads lighter. But the next day the horses could barely carry the empty pack saddles so they loaded all the supplies on the little mule. They knew the horses would be needed to help carry the children out.

The next day they passed the grave of another of the men who had died, as well as the unburied body they had seen on the way out.

They knew they had four or five more days of travel if they continued on the trail they had used to come out. Still worried that the emigrants would quit waiting and try to escape alone, they decided on a shortcut. Before that day ended they were forced to abandon both horses, as they could no longer keep the animals moving. Both men wept until they could no longer hear the plaintive cries of the despairing horses. That night they camped by water, the first they had seen for two days.

The next night they camped at the first campsite they had used on the way out. Twenty-five days had passed, and they feared the emigrants had been killed by Indians or had tried to escape by some other route, as they saw no sign of travelers at the campsite. The next forenoon they saw the unburied body of another emigrant who had joined the Bennett-Arcan group shortly before they left.

In fact, three wagons of other men had joined the group before Manly and Rogers left, so they hoped to see seven wagons on their return. About noon they could make out the remains of four wagons. Approaching closer they saw that the canvas covers had been stripped off the wagons, and they could see no oxen or any sign of life. The two men grieved, sure now that their life and death struggle to go out and return had been in vain and wondering if they could escape a second time.

Then they saw a man appear, throw his hands over his head and shout, "The boys have come! The boys have come."

Bennett and Arcan came forward as fast as they could move. The men embraced Manly and Rogers, and Sarah Bennett fell to her knees and clung to Rogers — himself a skin-covered skeleton — "like a maniac in the great emotion that came to her, and not a word was spoken." A long time passed before the people could talk without weeping.

All the people in the Bennett and Arcan wagons had survived. Bennett explained that he had tried to get the other three wagons to stay, but those people left saying, "If those boys ever get out of this cussed hole, they'd be damned fools to ever come back."

They took four oxen on the trip out, one for each woman, one for water, and one for the four children. They used the wagon covers to make saddles so the children and women could ride. They could only take the clothing they wore, so the women and children put on their best finery. Abigail Arcan had a beautiful hat and she even cut some extra ribbon for it. It streamed out behind her as the emaciated woman — by then five months pregnant — rode her ox out of the place where she and her family had nearly died. Her baby Julia, born the next July, lived only nineteen days.

After the Bennetts and the Arcans were safely in Southern California, Rogers went north to prospect and Manly soon followed. After Rogers suffered mercury poisoning resulting in partial amputations of both feet, he settled in Merced. Manly did well at prospecting, returned east, and then came back west to stay. He settled in San Jose and married. He and Rogers, who never married, visited and corresponded with each other. Manly died of heart failure in 1903, aged 83. Rogers died three years later, aged 84. Nearly blind and a patient in the county hospital, he slashed himself to death with his safety razor.

This story of two of California's greatest unsung heroes had an interesting sequel. In late 1861 Bennett and a small party abandoned sixty-year-old Charles Alvord as they were prospecting in Death Valley. Upon learning of the heartless action, Manly insisted that a rescue party go back in for Alvord. Bennett agreed, so he, Manly, and a third man, Caesar Twitchell, went back into Death Valley and found Alvord still alive.

The four decided that Manly and Alvord would continue prospecting while Bennett and Twitchell went out for more supplies. It snowed, and Bennett again abandoned Alvord and Alvord's rescuer, Manly, the man who had once rescued Bennett and his family from certain death. Bennett convinced Twitchell that the two men had either frozen to death or had escaped on their own.

Manly escaped death in Death Valley for the third time. By his refusal to leave an injured man behind, he saved Alvord as well, just as he and Rogers had saved the ungrateful Bennett a few years before. Manly was a good and honest man.

Suggested Reading: William Lewis Manly, *Death Valley in '49* (San Jose: The Pacific Tree and Vine Co., 1894).

KEEP YOUR SEAT, HORACE

Horace Greeley headed west in 1859 to see what his famous advice — Go West, young man, go West — had brought about. His stage reached Carson City on July 29. Hank Monk stepped up to drive the rest of the way to Placerville.

Monk, thirty-three, had been born in New York. He loved horses and once had driven eight-horse teams in the streets of Boston. He came around Cape Horn in 1852 to San Francisco, where he soon found work driving stages between Sacramento and Auburn. By 1859 he was driving between Carson City and Placerville for the Pioneer Stage Line. A flamboyant man, he took great pride in his driving ability. No one could handle six horses better on narrow mountain roads than he.

Monk's stage stopped at Woodford's, just across the state line, for the night. Greeley had agreed to lecture in Placerville the next day. When he boarded the stage the next morning, he told Monk he was worried about arriving in time. He wanted to be in Placerville by five, and it was one hundred nine miles away.

"I'll get you there," Monk said.

Greeley, founder and editor of the *New York Tribune* who had served in Congress and would later run for president, wrote about the precipitous cliffs on the right as they climbed the narrow road cut into the side of the Sierra Nevada Mountains.

"Yet along this mere shelf," he wrote, "with hardly a place in each mile where two meeting wagons can pass, the mail stage was driven as fast as wild California horses could draw it. Our driver was, of course, skillful, but had he met a wagon suddenly on rounding one of the sharp points or projections we were constantly passing, a fearful crash was unavoidable."

Two years later Monk gave his version to Samuel Clemens, a young reporter who had just joined the Virginia City *Territorial Enterprise* and would later become famous as Mark Twain.

"I looked into the coach and there was Greeley," Monk said, "his bare head bobbing, sometimes on the back and then on the front seat, sometimes in the coach and then out, then on the top and then on the bottom, holding on to whatever he could grab. Presently someone touched me on the back. 'Driver,' said a voice, 'I'm not particular about an hour or two!' 'Horace,' says I, 'keep your seat! I told you I would get you there by five o'clock, and by God I'll do it, if the axles hold!' And I did."

A terrified Greeley was delighted to see the reception committee at Sportsman's Hall, the last station before Placerville. While Monk changed horses, Greeley fled to the reception committee's lighter carriage. "I'll ride the rest of the way with them," he shouted to Monk. "They'll get there before you."

"We'll see," Monk replied.

When Greeley reached his hotel in Placerville, he told the proprietor to let him know when Monk's stage got in. Monk stepped up to his side.

"I've been waiting an hour and a half, Horace."

Greeley took Monk up the street and bought him the best suit of clothes he could find.

Twenty years later, President Grant on an around-the-world tour specially requested that Hank Monk transport him from Lake Tahoe to Carson City.

"Hank, if you can't drive the team," Grant said, "just hand me the ribbons."

"General, I'll get you there safe and on time."

And he did. Monk let the president hold the reins for a few minutes.

"You may be a tolerable good fellow to run a government," Hank said, taking back the reins. "But I'm damned if you was cut out for a stage driver."

The following year, President Rutherford B. Hayes toured the West Coast, the first president to do so during his term of office. He also had Hank Monk drive him between Carson City and Lake Tahoe. His route was westbound, the opposite of Grant's.

"This is pretty steep," Hayes said. "Do we have to walk?"

"Keep your seat, Mister Hayes, I'll get you there on time."

A heavy drinker throughout his career, Monk became an alcoholic at the end. He enjoyed sitting in the Ormsby House saloon in Carson City and telling stories of his experiences driving presidents and near-presidents. The stories got better as the years went on. But no one has ever shown or claimed more skill at driving stages down hairpin mountain grades at breakneck speeds. He never had an accident.

Monk is buried in Lone Mountain Cemetery in Carson City, not far from the grave of Snowshoe Thompson, who was also renowned for his skillful and breakneck descents down mountains. Thompson did it with long narrow boards, later called skis, strapped to his feet. Monk used six barely broken horses. Both were equally daring and nonchalant.

Suggested reading: Rich Pitter, *Hank Monk: He'll Get You There on Time* (South Lake Tahoe: Lake Tahoe Historical Society, 1995).

HANK MONK

Nevada Historical Society

CLAIM DENIED

A September, 1838, Indian raid on a packtrain near the Santa Fe Trail and the resulting claim against the government provide a revealing look at the hazards of early-day packing and government attempts to protect its citizens against hostile Indians.

The train, belonging to Bent, St. Vrain & Co., was led by Marcelen St, Vrain. With three horses, nine mules, and six men, it left Bent's Fort on the north bank of the Arkansas River in present Colorado bound for Santa Fe. Pawnee Indians attacked along a tributary, some distance south of the main stream.

A man named Crawford was killed. Blass Grego and Rafael Sanchez were wounded. Sebastiano Xaninellio, Santes Padico, and the train commander were unhurt.

The Pawnees were led by Big Soldier. He thought the whites were Spaniards. In his deposition, submitted in support of the traders' claim, he said he felt sorry when he later learned that "these white men were not Spaniards, but my white American brothers."

The twelve animals carried 23 buffalo robes, 25 pounds of sugar and 25 pounds of steel, 38 pairs of brogans, three guns and 10 pounds of balls, 15 pounds of coffee, a camp kettle and an axe, 25 pounds of printer's ink, eight Spanish bridles, two Latin missals, ten reams of paper, and an assortment of calico, domestics, moleskin, and scarlet cloth.

The claim included $100 for each horse and packsaddle lost and $75 for each mule and packsaddle lost. It also asked $40 for the rifle taken from Crawford and $75 for three guns taken (probably pistols). The claim added up to $3273. Besides Big Soldier's, it also had a supporting deposition from the wounded Blass Grego.

The traders' claim was forwarded to John Dougherty, agent for the Pawnee Tribe. He presented it to the tribal council, where Big Soldier admitted the attack. Dougherty resigned shortly after, saying he thought he had sent the claim on for payment to the Commissioner of Indian Affairs in May, 1839.

Dougherty was succeeded by a Mr. Hamilton, whose habits "entirely disqualified him from attending to the duties of his office." Five years later the claim papers were found in a box belonging to Hamilton but in the possession of a captain of dragoons. The captain turned them over, and they were sent on to Washington.

The Commissioner of Indian Affairs said the claim was legitimate, but could not be paid. The government's annuity to the tribe was paid in goods, not money. There was nothing to deduct the $3273 from. The commissioner added that he thought some of the prices claimed for lost items were "enormously" high.

The agent for the traders supplemented the claim with affidavits from Alexander Papin and Michelle Robidouux that all the amounts claimed were usual and customary in that part of the country for the properties lost. Then he submitted the claim directly to Congress.

The Congressional Committee on Indian Affairs immediately asked the commissioner if the attack had occurred within United States territory. The Arkansas River was the boundary between United States territory and land claimed by Mexico. The Indians had attacked *between* the Arkansas River and the Spanish Settlements, but it was not on territory claimed by the United States..

The Committee on Indian Affairs denied the claim on March 3, 1845, almost seven years after the attack. It pointed out that the 1834 legislation to regulate trade with Indian tribes and preserve peace on the frontier made the government the guarantor to any citizen damaged by Indian depredations. But since the robbery occurred outside the United States, the government had no responsibility to the damaged traders.

Certainly the traders were sorry they had lost a man, their animals and equipment, and their trade goods. The Pawnees said they were sorry they had attacked their white brothers by mistake. We don't know how the committee members felt.

Suggested reading: House Report No. 194, H.R. 28th Congress, 2d Sess, March 3, 1845.

CAMELS IN THE CARIBOO

The gold discovered in the Cariboo Mountains of British Columbia in the late 1850s had to be freighted through three hundred fifty miles of rough country from Quesnel and Barkerville to Fort Yale on the Fraser River. Following narrow trails that wound across steep slopes above the river meant that mules packing two hundred pounds could only travel about fifteen miles a day. Freighter Frank Laumeister thought there should be a better way. He knew the United States Army had been experimenting with camels to carry freight across the southwest deserts from Texas to California. So he took a steamer to San Francisco to see if any surplus animals were available.

He found something better. The army had been using dromedary (single hump) camels from Africa and the Middle East. They could cover thirty or forty miles each day while carrying six hundred pounds, but the Bactrian (double hump) camels from the deserts of Asia could carry a thousand pounds the same distances. Furthermore the Bactrian camels were more used to the cold weather they would find in the north.

Otto Esche of San Francisco had already figured this out, and he had imported three shiploads of the animals from Mongolia and Manchuria. Unfortunately several of the animals had died during their three-month voyage across the Pacific, and he was willing to sell some to recover part of his investment. Laumeister bought twenty-three for six thousand dollars.

One camel escaped while being transferred to a northbound steamer and another died on the voyage to Canada, but Laumeister unloaded the other twenty-one at Fort Victoria on April 14, 1862. He reloaded them on a paddle-wheeler going upriver to Fort Yale, supply center for the Cariboo mines.

The day the little paddle-wheeler steamed into Fort Yale always brought spectators, wondering what new people, what new things were coming in from the outside world. Their numbers were larger than usual that bright spring morning in May because they had heard about the arrival of the camels. Probably very few, if any, had ever seen one outside a school book picture. These misshapen beasts certainly seemed big enough and strong enough to carry a half ton. And their thick fur coats from the cold winters of northern Asia indicated no trouble with Canadian cold.

But no one anticipated the two main qualities of these strange visitors from a half-world away. First, their disposition. These camels had been driven hundreds of miles to the sea from their home ranges in Manchuria and Mongolia. Then followed the long months of being cooped up on a rolling, pitching ship, where several of their number died, perhaps from seasickness. They had little time to enjoy the stable land by San Francisco harbor — although long enough that one of their number decided to make the enjoyment permanent and escaped — before they were loaded again on a smaller, more crowded ship for another long passage north. And if that wasn't enough to accelerate an ingrained disposition toward ugliness, they were again loaded up on an even smaller ship for their trip up river. They came off the little paddle-wheeler in Fort Yale kicking, hissing, and spitting on everyone they could reach.

But more alarming than that, especially for those who got too close and had to dodge flying feet and wipe off gobs of spittle and snot, was the sudden realization that *everyone* in Yale was too close to these animals. Never had anyone smelled anything like them before. Bear scat during breeding season, and moose meat left in the sun until it became a maggot-infested, putrid pile were *Eau de Cologne* in comparison. Some people gagged, fearful that breathing deeply would make them throw up. And it wasn't just the people. Pack mules along the waterfront curled their upper lips, waved their ears, and looked around disdainfully, wondering what calamity had infested their orderly world.

One of the mules was too close, but before he could escape the stench, the vile-tempered camels first off the boat charged him with slashing hooves and biting teeth and killed the poor creature before the stunned bystanders could rescue him. Laumeister and his packers finally got the camels under control, and he paid off the irate owner of the deceased mule.

But the real problems came with the behavior of the camels on the trail. Whenever horses, oxen, or mules came near, the anti-social camels attacked, and the other freighting or packing animals bolted. Before long, entire pack trains had plunged off canyon trails and mountainsides along with their valuable loads of freight. The Dromedary Express, as it was mistakenly called, was soon feared and hated all along the Cariboo Road.

One day Laumeister sat in a Fort Yale saloon, dejected with his almost total loss of friends. "I'm willing to try anything you can suggest," he announced to other freighters in the room.

"How about givin' them stinkin' devils a bath?" someone suggested.

"Yeah. Plenty of strong lye soap oughta de-skunk 'em," another man added.

"What them critters need is some strong perfoom," a third wit suggested.

The crowd in the saloon took up the cry. "O de Colonee, that's what you spray 'em with, Frank."

They passed the hat, took up a collection, and soon a package of *Eau de Cologne* reached Fort Yale. It was a good try and the men had a few laughs, but nature had endowed the camels with an odor that mere men could not overcome.

Laumeister also learned that the flinty rocks on the trail tore at his camels' hooves and cut them up so much the camels were badly lamed at the end of a 700-mile round trip.

Losses to other freighters and packers continued to mount. The most treacherous part of the Cariboo Road was in the Fraser River Canyon, just south of Quesnel. There George Hilton, a young teamster freighting up from Fort Yale with a twelve-horse team, met five camels coming south. When the wind out of the north brought the scent, Hilton's horses plunged into a frenzy. Young George desperately yanked the reins as his horses thundered along the narrow, precipitous road. But the struggle was hopeless. The lead horses suddenly slipped off the road, pulling the rest of the team after them. George was able to save himself by leaping from the wagon into a solid rock wall which knocked him unconscious. He was spared the death cries of his horses as they hurtled into the churning water of the Fraser River far below.

"My God, it's happened again," said one of Laumeister's freighters when they came upon Hilton's prostrate form in the trail. They got him on a camel and took him to Fort Yale where he recovered from his many injuries, including a broken leg. But he also sued Laumeister for the loss of his freighting outfit. Laumeister, a fair man, paid him off, but it was just one claim among many.

Finally a petition was signed by irate freighters and sent to the governor at Victoria, the capital of the newly-formed province. They demanded that Laumeister take his camels off the road, and that they be driven out of the country. Laumeister resigned from freighting. He turned the camels loose in the mountains near Kamloops and moved to San Francisco.

It was reported that Laumeister fell off a ferry in San Francisco harbor about fourteen years later and drowned. For about forty years, a camel would be seen from time to time in southern British Columbia. After 1906 no such reports were made. It was speculated that they fell prey to grizzlies. Perhaps they also caused some consternation to the moose in the area. They certainly added an interesting chapter to packing on northern trails

Suggested reading: Olive F. Spencer, "Cariboo's Dromedary Express" in *Frontier Times.* August-September, 1967.

ARMY TEAMSTER

Sam Stringer was a thirty-year old teamster for the Confederate Army when he was captured at the Battle of Wilson Creek in 1861. Sam, from North Carolina, didn't feel strongly about the South's position in the Civil War; he just wanted his six-mule team back. He went to the Yankee commander, told him the mules were all he had in the world, and that he needed a job.

"I'll be glad to work for you Yanks, if you need a teamster," Sam said.

The commander took Sam up on the offer and released him and his mules from custody. At war's end Sam was driving mules for the 18th Infantry at Fort Leavenworth, Kansas.

When Colonel Carrington came through in Spring 1866 to build a fort in Wyoming, Sam Stringer joined up. The expedition reached the forks of the Piney River in July and began building Fort Phil Kearny. Sam hauled logs to the fort from the sawmill, set up six miles west in Big Piney Canyon.

Indians, resenting white encroachment on their hunting grounds, harassed the logging camp, but Sam survived the summer and fall uninjured.

The climax came on December 21, the last trip for the wood train that winter. Sam had to stay in the fort and repair his wagon, so he was not with the train. When Indians attacked the train, a relief column under Captain Fetterman rode out. Fetterman did not return to the fort, and Carrington ordered another detail under Captain Ten Eyck to ride to Fetterman's assistance.

Sam admired Captain Fred Brown, a member of Fetterman's command with whom he had worked, and he was concerned about Brown's safety.

"He was the whitest man I ever worked for," Sam said as he begged Ten Eyck to let him take his wagon with the detail. Ten Eyck agreed.

They found forty-nine bodies of Fetterman's command.

"I can never put in words the sorrow that I felt when I found the body of Captain Brown and realized that my friend was lost to me forever," Sam said. He hauled the forty-nine bodies back to the fort.

The next day another detail found thirty-two more bodies, the rest of Fetterman's command. Sam also drove his wagon with that detail.

Sam Stringer missed the Wagon Box fight, but he was with the supply train for General George Crook in his 1876 campaign against the Sioux. He worked at Camp Carlin, near Cheyenne, until 1898, when he returned to Johnson County, remaining there until his death in 1905.

Suggested reading: Lorah B. Chaffin, *Sons of the West* (Caldwell: The Caxton Printers, 1941).

APPRECIATION

Bob Emery was only a boy when he followed older brother Charley to employment on the Overland Mail. Hired as a stock tender, Bob wanted to become a stage driver. When the drivers pulled in to the station for a quick change of horses, Bob always made sure the fresh team was ready.

Bob knew the company appreciated Charley when it promoted him to station keeper. Then Bob got his chance to drive, and he hoped the company would appreciate him, too.

Indian trouble began when the soldiers guarding the trail were sent east to fight the Civil War. Sometimes, as Bob drove, he would imagine that mounted Indians suddenly appeared on a ridge ahead. Then he would carefully think out how he could protect his passengers and mail. Bob yearned to become the best driver on the line, so he could earn the respect and appreciation that Charley had.

Bob, small in size, was in awe of the stageline's owner, Ben Holladay. This huge man with the booming voice often boasted about the meals served at the stations. Bob was proud that Mary, Charley's wife, was singled out by Holladay for his highest compliment. One day the stage pulled in to Charley's station with Holladay aboard. Mary served Holladay's favorite meal, and the story traveled up and down the line of how Holladay leaned back, patted his stomach, and tossed a twenty-dollar gold piece to the beaming cook.

"By God," he roared, "that was a Jim Dandy feed! You keep the change, now. Understand?"

Twenty dollars! Almost a month's pay for most men! Now, that was appreciation!

Bob was at Atchison, Kansas, the eastern end of the line, when reports came in August, 1864, of new Indian attacks. The Indians were attacking all the way from Julesburg to Charley's Liberty Farm Station. Bob ran to the stage office and asked how soon he could get out, either as a driver or passenger.

"Hell, sonny, you kin drive tomorry's stage if'n you want. The older drivers ain't askin' to go. They got too much sense fer that.""

Bob pulled out on August 8 with a four-horse stage and nine passengers. The next morning he dropped down to the Little Blue River and pulled into Big Sandy Station. He had covered 140 miles; he still had fifty-three miles to go.

After a quick breakfast, Bob hurried his passengers back into the coach and shouted at his fresh team. Both driver and passengers were grim and quiet as they moved along the river. Bob stopped to change teams at Thompson and Kiowa Stations. The attendant at Kiowa warned him that Indians had been seen east of Liberty Farm.

"Watch for the narrows, Bob," he said. "That's where they'll hit if they come east of Little Blue."

The Narrows, about eight miles ahead, was a place where the road was squeezed between the river and thirty-foot high bluffs. It would be impossible to see an ambush.

Bob was anxious to reach his brother's station, twenty-five miles away, but he kept the horses in check. If he had to call on them for extra speed, he wanted it available. He passed a 25-wagon ox train, conducted by George Constable.

"Seen any Indians?" shouted Bob.

"Nary a one so far," replied Constable.

Just past the Eubanks ranch, about 150 yards from the Narrows, Bob saw the screaming Indians riding toward him. He quickly swung the team around and whipped them to full speed. Pushing his team to its limit, he hoped he would not get hit badly enough to lose control. When Constable saw the stage approaching, he had his bullwhackers circle the wagons, leaving room for the stage to enter.

After one of the West's wildest stage rides, Bob reached the circled wagons. By then the stage bristled with arrows "like quills upon a fretful porcupine." Parts of a harness were shot away, but miraculously no one was hurt. The Indians rode back to the Eubanks ranch and killed the rancher and captured his wife and baby. Bob was relieved to learn that, although the Liberty Farm Station was burned to the ground, neither Charley nor Mary were hurt.

Bob Emery never enjoyed robust health. A year later, as he lay dying from fever, a Mrs. Randolph came to him. She slipped a ring on his finger after reading to Bob the message engraved inside:

E. Umphry, G.C. Randolph, and Hattie P. Randolph to ROBERT EMERY, in acknowledgment of what we owe to his cool conduct and good driving on Tuesday, August 9, 1864.

Bob smiled. Now he, too, had his appreciation.

Suggested reading: Frank A. Root & William E. Connelley, *The Overland Stage to California* (Columbus: College Book, 1950).

EXTRA DUTY FOR TEAMSTERS & PACKERS

Sometimes teamsters and packers hauled more than freight, mail, and people. During the Montana gold rush, when road agents preyed on lives and property under the secret supervision of the sheriff, wagon trains and pack trains also furnished protection for those carrying out gold.

In late November, 1863, Milton S. Moody's three-wagon train, traveling along with a pack train, left Virginia City for Salt Lake City. Moody had been freighting on this road since the initial discovery on Grasshopper Creek a year before. This time, however, one of his wagons held a carpet bag filled with $1500 in greenbacks hidden in letters addressed to various people in the states.

But the main treasure was $80,000 worth of gold dust in saddle bags distributed among the pack saddles of the pack train. The businessmen who had purchased the dust rode along with the pack train, hoping to get their fortune to Salt Lake City for deposit in banks. Well aware of the community suspicion that Henry Plummer, their sheriff, was a secret lookout for robbers, the men were all well armed and prepared for trouble.

In fact, Plummer was in charge of the road agents and had picked two of the best, Dutch John Wagner and Steve Marshland, to hold up the combined wagon and pack trains. They followed the trains in bitterly cold weather as they crossed Stinking Water Creek and made their second camp site at Black Tail Deer Canyon.

There the robbers crawled through a thicket to spy on the teamsters and packers after they had their camp set up. Dutch John proposed that they kill four men with shotgun fire as soon as it was dark and then, by shouting, fast moving, and rapid firing they would convince the rest that they faced a large force and they would run.

"Then we'll have plenty of time to go through their stuff," Dutch John said. But Marshland, noting that their victims seemed to stay awfully close to their rifles as they huddled around their fires, was unwilling, and they returned to their mounts and waited until morning.

In the morning the campers heard noises from two approaching riders, and each one instantly grabbed his rifle or revolver, ready to fire. Then, Dutch John and Marshland rode nonchalantly into the camp, each with a shotgun across his saddle. When they saw every man ready to fight, they smiled innocently and inquired if the party had seen any horses running at large. When the teamsters said they had no extra horses, the road agents moved on.

Two days later, December 4, the combined trains approached the ridge dividing Red Rock Creek from Junction Creek. The pack train went on ahead to select a stopping place for the night. To the two robbers watching from a distance, it appeared that only Moody and two teamsters were left with the wagons. As soon as the packers were out of sight, Dutch John and Marshland rode down and held up the wagon train.

Dutch John held his rifle on the three men while Marshland searched the train for the gold dust. He found the bag of greenbacks but, of course, no gold. He did not know until he got to the rear wagon that it contained two of the Virginia City business men, Lank Forbes and another who was sick and being cared for by Forbes. When Marshland stepped up on the double tree of the rear wagon, Forbes shot him in the chest with his single-shot dragoon pistol. Dutch John's mule reared from the loud noise, sending his two-barrel shotgun blast over the heads of the teamsters. Marshland fell to the frozen ground and staggered back to his feet. He was able to run into the pine woods and escape, but the teamsters confiscated his horse, along with his weapons, provisions, and twenty pounds of tea that Marshland had stolen from another train a few days before. Dutch John escaped on his mule, but Moody drew a revolver from his boot and shot him in the shoulder as he galloped away.

When the wagon train reached the pack train camp, three of the packers rode back and followed Marshland's trail until near midnight. They recovered all the greenbacks but didn't find Marshland, although they learned later that they had come within fifteen feet of him.

On the remainder of the trip to Salt Lake City, the wagon train men discussed the division of their booty. Forbes thought he should have Marshland's horse and what it carried as it was his shot that foiled the robbery attempt. Moody thought he had a claim as he had wounded Dutch John. Drawing on an analogy from sea pirates, the two teamsters claimed a share as they were in sight when the prize was captured. They finally elected a judge, impaneled a jury, and decided for Forbes, provided he paid thirty dollars to Moody and twenty to each teamster. They probably drank the tea on the road.

On December 21, Montana vigilantes, determined to stop the rash of robberies and killings, hanged George Ives. He had been a packer in Washington Territory and British Columbia before he turned to crime. He and Marshland had held up a stage in November, before the robbery of the Moody train, and he had killed a popular young man in early December.

Ives' execution made Dutch John nervous. With an unhealed shoulder wound, he feared being identified as an attacker of the Moody train. He went to Henry Plummer with his fears, and Plummer advised him to get out of the Territory. Dutch John and a Bannack Indian rode toward Salt Lake.

John X. Beidler, who had officiated at Ives' execution, rode down the

Salt Lake road to meet a train at the Snake River. He rode back with it to Beaverhead Valley, where he learned about the robbery of the Moody train and got a description of Dutch John and Marshland.

Shortly after, Beidler met Dutch John and the Indian in Beaver Canyon, but did not recognize them. The weather was still bitterly cold, down to thirty below or colder at nights. Beidler offered Dutch John a drink but the robber's hands were so badly frozen he could not hold the bottle. They spent the night together on the trail, and Beidler soaked and dressed Dutch John's hands for him.

The next day Dutch John was recognized by two packers in a train bound for Salt Lake, but holed up in camp as it was too cold to travel. The packers saw Dutch John and the Indian take shelter in a vacant cabin. They went immediately to John Fetherstun, who was also camped nearby with eight teams and drivers. Fetherstun said the robber should be hanged from a projecting log at the cabin. That justice was too sudden for the two packers. They went on down the road to the camp of Neil Howie. He was returning from Salt Lake with three ox-drawn wagons filled with groceries and flour. They couldn't have found a better man.

Born in Scotland and raised in Wisconsin, Howie was brave as a lion. Howie's three teamsters promised to help him, but when Dutch John and the Indian appeared on the road, traveling toward them, they backed down.

"You got any tobacco?" Dutch John asked Howie.

"None to spare. But there's a big train following and they'll have some."

Casting a suspicious glance at Howie's teamsters, the robber rode on. Howie waited until Dutch John was almost out of sight and then rode rapidly after him. When he caught up, both Dutch John and the Indian were ready to fight. But Howie, slowing only enough to be heard, shouted, "I need to borrow a shoeing hammer from that big train to get some bulls ready to cross the divide."

The robbers watched him ride on.

But none of the men in the big train, when Howie reached it, wanted to have anything to do with capturing Dutch John.

"But it's a burning shame, a reproach to the Territory, and an eternal reproach to us to let so great a villain escape," Howie pleaded. "He's a horse thief and a murderer, stained with blood."

The teamsters in the big train were still shaking their heads when Dutch John and the Indian rode into sight.

"You got any tobacco?" the fugitive asked.

"You got any money?"

"Not a cent."

"Then we have no tobacco."

"Oh, let him have it," Howie said. "I'll pay for it."

With a grateful expression, Dutch John rode on. Neil made another appeal to the teamsters to not let the road agent escape. They said nothing doing.

"Then I'll do it myself."

He shouted after Dutch John, "Hey captain, wait up a minute."

Dutch John wheeled his mule around and waited as Neil approached. The fugitive was a large man, his face hardened by crime. His eyes beamed malice as the smaller man walked toward him. Neil's gray eyes were clear and calm, and the hand on his revolver was steady. Dutch John held his rifle in both hands as if preparing for a deadly aim. For an instant it seemed that one of the weapons would decide the issue. Then the robber quailed before Howie's determined gaze. Howie walked closer, laid his hand on the mule's flank and said, quietly, "Give me your gun and get off your mule."

With a pale face and trembling hands, Dutch John complied.

Howie took his prisoner back to his train which was still in camp because of the cold. Many of his oxen had died from exposure, and others would lose part of their hooves and tails by spring.

When he and Dutch John were warmed up by the fire, Howie said, "I arrested you for robbing Moody's train last month."

"I had nothing to do with it."

"That's easy to tell. The man they said was you got shot in the shoulder. Take off your shirt and we'll have a look."

"In spite of the cold the shirt came off, and Dutch John said the wound had been caused by an accidental discharge of his pistol as he had lain too close to his campfire."

Howie placed a pistol cap near the fire until it exploded. "That shows it couldn't be true," he said. "You would have been on fire before the shot went off."

Howie couldn't find a man among fifty or sixty teamsters who was willing to help him take Dutch John into Bannack. Then he found John Fetherstun who jumped at the chance. But it was still so cold they kept Dutch John for two days in the same vacant cabin he had used earlier, and then they took him to Bannack.

It was still so cold they had to stop every few miles to build a fire and warm up. After three days of travel and thwarting three attempts by their prisoner to escape, they reached Bannack, where Howie told Sheriff Plummer he had the man in custody for the Moody Wagon Train holdup.

"I'll take him off your hands," Plummer said, "and relieve you of all further responsibility."

"Not exactly, Plummer. I'll keep him until the people's tribunal decides what to do. I had a good deal of trouble bringing him in, and don't intend to let him escape."

Fetherstun kept Dutch John a prisoner in a cabin in Yankee Flat on the outskirts of Bannack. Under questioning by the vigilantes, Dutch John confessed and implicated several other road agents in other holdups of wagon and pack trains. One night the two men could hear approaching footsteps and suppressed voices outside. Fearing an attempt to capture his prisoner by the road agents, Fetherstun got his guns ready for defense. Then he saw Dutch John doing the same. The prisoner could have shot his keeper, but he feared the vengeance of his comrades more than the justice of the vigilantes. The men outside, aware that the two inside were ready, withdrew.

Dutch John was hanged on January 11, the day after the vigilantes hanged Sheriff Henry Plummer. On January 16 the vigilantes found Steve Marshland in a ranch cabin on the Big Hole River, where he was laid up with frozen feet. He denied robbing the Moody Train but had no explanation for the bullet wound in his chest. He was hanged from a long pole, projecting across a corral fence.

Fetherstun and Howie liked their experience in law enforcement more than being teamsters and packers. Fetherstun was soon a principal assistant to John X. Beidler as more road agents were brought to a rough and sudden justice.

Later that spring the territorial governor appointed Howie sheriff of Madison County. From there he became the first deputy United States marshal for Montana. In the early 1870s, when he was about forty, Howie was assistant superintendent of a Remington mining operation in Trinidad, off the coast of South America. One day on that job he was riding with a pack train when it was attacked by rebels. Howie killed a sergeant and a lieutenant in defending that attack. Later he shot a rebel captain to death in a saloon. He died of malaria a few months later.

Suggested reading: Nathaniel Pitt Langford, *Vigilante Days and Ways* (1890).

FREIGHTING IN MONTANA

In 1865 Alexander Toponce made four round trips hauling freight between Fort Union and Helena , 450 miles apart on the Missouri river in northern Montana Territory. As Toponce's bullwhackers traveled the 3600 miles with oxen traveling about twelve miles a day, they fought Indians, witnessed two murders, and suffered through one of the worst blizzards in Montana history.

Toponce, a twenty-five-year-old Frenchman, had come to the United States when he was six years old. At fifteen he moved on west to whack bulls for Russell Majors and Waddell. After driving stage on the Santa Fe Trail, riding for the Pony Express, and serving as a wagon boss for the army in the Mormon War, he tried his luck in the Colorado Gold Rush. The luck was bad, but he moved on to Montana where he made twenty thousand dollars mining and spent the money buying his own freight outfit.

Toponce left Helena on his first trip in April, 1865, with a government contract to haul freight back from Fort Union. On the trip down river with empty wagons, they hitched two or three yoke of oxen to a wagon, sometimes chaining three or four wagons together. So most of the oxen were driven along in a herd at the rear of the train, and at least half the men could rest each day.

The freighters' road lay on the north side of the Missouri River, crossing open meadows between the fringe of timber at the river and the high bluffs to the north.

At Fort Union they loaded coffee, sugar, blankets, and other supplies for the Indians. They had little trouble on the first trip, as the Indians knew the freight was coming for them. Toponce hauled some of the supplies on to Helena from Fort Benton. Reading between the lines, it appears that those supplies were stolen by the Indian agent and sold for his own benefit to merchants in Helena.

They hauled freight both ways on the second trip. Going down to Fort Union they carried buffalo hides, which the Indian agent had bought from the Indians for shipment down river to St. Louis.

Maintaining regular military discipline on the second trip, they traveled in two lines of wagons, about fifty or seventy-five feet apart. They could form the wagons into a circle, with the oxen safely inside, on about five minutes' notice. Since they had had no Indian trouble on the first trip, several other trains also decided to freight goods, and Toponce traveled with six other trains as they returned from Fort Union. The trains traveled and camped about a half mile apart, close enough to help each other out, but not so close that their oxen, grazing in the evening, would get mixed together.

The Indian problems started on the third trip. This time Toponce had borrowed two howitzers from the army at Fort Benton. When Indians approached within a mile of the trains, Toponce would fire the howitzers, forcing the Indians to keep their distance.

Toponce had about sixty men. Each carried a single-shot Smith & Wesson rifle on his back, a revolver in his belt, and a sixteen shot Henry rifle in his wagon. When they were a little east of Wolf Point on the way back, a band of 250 to 300 warriors attacked. The bullwhackers, their wagons closed into a circle, killed or wounded at least fifty Indians without losing a man.

It was a hot, dry day in late September, they only had one small keg of water, and they were corraled about a mile from the river. The Indians kept them under siege, so the bullwhackers worked all night digging a well. By morning they were down fifteen feet with barely enough water for cooking and their own drinking. They escorted the oxen to the river in groups of ten or twelve, with armed men surrounding them. The Indians finally rode off.

This third trip completed Toponce's contract with the government, so he sold his train. But he learned that 400 tons of army supplies had been stored in Fort Union, and the soldiers there were being transferred down river to Fort Rice. The government had decided to sell the supplies.

Toponce paid forty thousand dollars for forty wagons and 405 oxen and started back to Fort Union with his new train, this time speculating on buying goods to be resold in Helena. He still had the borrowed howitzers for protection. Other trains, including one owned by Jerry Mann, also headed down river, expecting to haul some of the freight back.

Toponce had his train loaded at Fort Union by December 24, but Mann asked him to wait until Mann was ready so they could travel together. Toponce agreed.

Further delay resulted when two of Mann's bullwhackers got drunk and attacked his night herder. The night herder killed both of them, and was arrested for murder. The trains waited for the trial.

The jury acquitted the herder, saying he acted in self defense. The trains moved out on January 1. A snowstorm struck them two days later, when they were about forty miles west of Fort Union.

They corraled their wagons and drove their oxen down to an old Indian camp on the river. The Indians had cut about a hundred cords of wood there the winter before. They had fed the bark to their horses and expected to return and pick up the remainder for firewood. But the bullwhackers got there first.

The cold was so severe that for fifteen days half the men stayed awake at all times. They kept fires going in the Sibley stoves inside their tents and also on the open ground between the tents. The horns on the oxen froze and burst open. Some animals froze to death as they were standing, too cold to move. By the end of ten days, the men had shot all the oxen still alive to take them out of their misery.

Buffalo began to crowd in. Those that couldn't find shelter in the timber froze to death. By spring a man could walk for miles on buffalo skeletons, his feet never touching the ground.

Mann's train had stopped about seven miles downstream, where the Quaking Asp River joined the Missouri. By the time he had lost all his oxen and horses, Toponce had also lost all his horses, in addition to his oxen. Toponce had saved two mules by keeping them in his tent, feeding them cottonwood bark and buffalo meat.

About the first of February Toponce and Mann started out for Helena, over four hundred miles away. They rode Toponce's two mules, planning to buy oxen and bring them back to take the trains on in. They couldn't carry anything except a pair of saddle blankets. Each night they killed a buffalo, skinned it, and lay the hide flesh-side down in the snow for their bed. All they had to eat was buffalo meat. All the mules had was cottonwood bark and buffalo meat. They chewed it just like hay.

After two hundred miles, they captured three Indian horses. This allowed them to travel faster, as the mules could get some rest. They turned the horses over to the Indian agent at Fort Benton, bought fresh horses and rode on to Helena, arriving March 9.

Toponce and Mann each bought a wagon and provisions, about twenty saddle animals — mules and horses — and about three hundred oxen. They each hired ten men and started back for the wagon trains on March 20.

About sixty miles before reaching Fort Benton, they ran into another snow storm. They herded the oxen into some timber along the Sun River so they would have shelter. They had their own camp set up on an island in the river about an hour after midnight.

The next morning about eight inches of new snow lay on the ground and some of their horses were missing. While bullwhackers looked for the horses, Toponce rode in a four-mile circle around their camp, looking for signs of Indians. He saw none, and the horses were found in a canyon, so that night when snow started falling again, they didn't mount a guard.

About four the next morning Molly, Toponce's favorite riding mule, was standing by his bed with an arrow in her leg. Toponce woke the rest of the men, shouting, "Well boys, it looks like we're afoot."

They found the tracks of five Indians in the snow, and all their horses were gone. They could see that the Indians had been huddled up in a grape thicket within one hundred yards of their camp. They had been there before the first snow started falling, and that is why Toponce saw no tracks in his wide circle. They could also tell that the Indians had been unable to keep Molly with the rest of the animals they stole, and they had finally shot her out of frustration.

It took four days for them to walk to Fort Benton, herding the oxen along on foot. Near Fort Benton two of their men were killed by Indians. In Fort Benton Toponce's wagon boss and Mann's wagon boss got into a fight, each one killing the other. These incidents delayed them another three or four days.

It was late in March when they reached the Marias, and both it and the Missouri were swollen from runoff. They tried to raft their provisions and wagons across the Marias, but the raft struck a large cottonwood tree and upset. One hundred fifty miles from Helena and still two hundred fifty from the train, they took a vote on whether to continue or return to Helena for more provisions. The men voted unanimously to continue.

Living again on buffalo meat, they moved on downstream toward the trains, Toponce riding Molly, Mann riding a horse, and the others driving the oxen on foot. They had a few skirmishes with Indians, and Toponce's wagon boss was killed by Blackfoot Indians after they had traveled about a hundred miles. They killed three of the Indian attackers and wounded another, who they turned over to Assiniboine Indians about fifteen miles further on. The Assiniboines tortured the wounded Blackfoot and then killed him.

When they reached the place where they had left Toponce's train, all they could find was part of one wagon caught high in a tree. When they reached Mann's train, seven miles below, they learned what had happened.

A warm chinook wind had melted snow and ice, sending a freezing flood down the Missouri River which swept everything away. Four of Toponce's men had been drowned. Fifteen more were badly crippled from clinging to treetops for sixty hours before they were rescued by friendly Indians and Mann's men. Mann's train had camped on higher ground, and they did not suffer so much.

Toponce's men said they had been sitting around their fire, barefooted, when they heard the roar of a fifty-foot wall of water and ice descending on them. One of Mann's men said it had been so cold they could not open a barrel of one hundred proof whiskey until they bored through several inches of ice.

Toponce's men had spent their time trapping wolves before the ice deluge. They had a thousand skins, all swept away in the flood.

Toponce arranged to send his crippled men on down river to Omaha. Then he and Mann returned upriver to Helena with their combined crews and Mann's train. Nothing was ever found of Toponce's train.

When Toponce left Helena about December 1 on his speculative trip to Fort Union he had his new train and about $75,000 in gold. When he got back on June 26 and paid off his men, all he had left was Molly, and he was eighteen dollars in the red. He borrowed $200, paid the balance of his debt, bought supplies, and rode Molly to Utah to start over.

When Toponce quit freighting he drove cattle to California, chased renegades, supplied beef to railroad crews, raced horses, ran a stage line in Idaho, ranched and ran a slaughter house, and served as mayor of Corinne, Utah. Still active at eighty, he wrote his reminiscences although he had never attended school one day in his life.

1865 was a year he remembered well.

Suggested reading: Alexander Toponce, Reminiscences (Norman: Univ of Oklahoma Press, 1971).

THESE WERE PERILOUS TIMES

Ben Arnold's mother died in childbirth, and his grandmother took him to raise but died when Ben was fourteen. After serving as cabin boy on a Cincinnati to St. Louis steamer, Ben enlisted in the Union Army at seventeen. He served three enlistments and then tried mining in Montana.

The cold and wet of mining troubled Ben, who suffered from bronchitis, and he became a night herder on Jerry Mann's freight line. In May, 1865, Mann's wagons went north from Helena to Fort Benton, arriving before the first boats came upriver from St. Louis. They took back a load of provisions and mining equipment that had been stored at Fort Benton the fall before.

Returning for another trip, they rested their oxen a few days on the trail and reached Fort Benton too late to get any freight from the upriver boats. Mann knew that a lot of freight had been off loaded at Fort Union the previous year, and he got a contract to pick some of it it up. The contract covered more freight than his train could carry, so Mann combined forces with the Matthews Brothers and Alexander Toponce. The trip to Fort Union was the fourth that season for Toponce. The three trains added up to 130 wagons, 150 men, and 1600 oxen.

Indians had been threatening, so Toponce obtained two government mountain howitzers, with charges of grape and cannister.

The three trains traveled about five miles apart, so their oxen would not get mixed up. Each train traveled in two parallel lines, a few rods apart, so they could corral quickly in case of attack. Ben didn't get to see much of the country, as night herders slept during the day in a wagon.

Meat was easy to find. A train's hunter could ride ahead and kill a buffalo almost any time and have it skinned out and ready to cut up by the time the train arrived. They preferred the tender meat from fat, dry cows. Hump roast was the best, but they also liked the liver and a kidney stew.

They saw few people other than Indians. Their hunter, Dutch John, traveled with his Arikara wife and their eight-year-old daughter. He was taking them back for a visit with relatives at Fort Berthold in Dakota Territory. A party of thirty Crow Indians traveled with them a while, and then turned south to steal horses from their enemies, the Teton Sioux. Ben learned later that the Sioux wiped out the Crows at a place called Rosebud Hill. They reached Fort Union in December. The last stream they crossed was frozen solid. They had been out of bread for a month.

Fort Union was a trading post on the north bank of the Missouri River, just west of the present North Dakota -Montana boundary. The gates

BEN ARNOLD

State Historical Society of North Dakota

were kept locked and barred at night to prevent Indian attack. Seven or eight wagons were allowed to enter at a time. As soon as they were loaded they pulled out, making way for the next group. Indians trading at the fort brought many horses, and grazing was poor. Loaded wagons were moved back up the river to wait, so the oxen would have better grazing. At that time of the year, the best grazing was still very poor.

As the train was about ready to start on the return trip, it had a short delay. Another of Mann's night herders, a man named Holmes with whom Ben had become pals, was attacked by two of Mann's bullwhackers, both drunk. Holmes killed them with a double-barreled shotgun. The men were buried at the fort and the train waited while Holmes was tried for murder.

Major David Pease, apparently an army officer, was chosen as judge. The improvised jury acquitted Holmes on grounds of self defense.

The return trip to Fort Benton started on January 1, 1866. Ben Arnold elected to not go, as his bronchitis was bothering him, and he missed one of the most exciting trips ever encountered by a freighting outfit in the west.

Arnold freighted with horses for several trips down river to Fort Berthold, a Northwest Fur Company post at the mouth of the Muddy (Little Missouri) River. He carried supplies down and brought furs back. One of his return loads was a shipment of eleven hundred buffalo tongues, salted and smoked for shipment to St. Louis in the spring. He carried oats for his horses but no hay. He turned the team loose in the evenings to eat cottonwood bark.

When the snow became too deep for horses, Arnold and several other unemployed men at Fort Union trapped and poisoned wolves. Wolf skins brought two dollars each; coyotes about half that. The Missouri River ice was three feet thick that winter.

By March the weather moderated and the trappers were able to skin the frozen wolf carcasses they had accumulated. But later that month a three-day blizzard with sixty-mile winds stormed in. They fired a six-pound howitzer to guide one of their men in from the trap line. At the end of the storm deer, buffalo, and elk walked on the top of drifted snow to graze on willow branches protruding up from below. It was the hardest winter Arnold had ever seen.

The camp of the wolfers was two abandoned cabins near the junction of the Yellowstone and the Missouri Rivers. Shortly after the blizzard, a chinook blew in and the warm winds turned the area into a wide torrent of floating chunks of ice carried along by the rising waters. Buffaloes, deer, elk, and smaller animals could be seen riding larger ice islands.

At first Arnold and a pal tried to escape the rising waters in the foggy darkness. Then they turned back to the buildings and took refuge with the others on the sod roofs, as ice chunks and islands swept by in the roiling waters.

Arnold had seen many Civil War battles, hearing the screeching of bullets and feeling the dirt flung into his face from those that came too close. But he never felt as near death as in that flood if ice. During the four day wait before they were rescued, the trappers perched on their cabin roofs of sod, wrapped in blankets and huddled around small fires.

Arnold went on down the Missouri River to Sioux City, where he looked forward to a change in diet. He was disappointed to learn that the main stay of his diet in the mountains — buffalo meat — was also the main food in that town.

Arnold cut wood for a time for steamboats, Then he married Itatewin, a Sioux girl from Wyoming. He had hired the girl to make clothing from the animal pelts he had got from hunting. (They had lost all their furs in the flooding during the chinook.) Arnold and Itatewin had a baby girl, whom they named Marcella.

A few years later, after driving a herd of cattle to the Cheyenne Agency, Arnold returned home to find his wife and child gone. He learned that she had heard he had been killed by a war party of Indians from Canada. Ben wrote, "I was grieved to find Itatewin and my baby gone, but these were perilous times and I could not blame my wife for acting on the rumor that had come to her."

When Marcella was five, Ben learned that Itatewin had married Charles McCarthy, a white trader at the Cheyenne Agency. Ben asked McCarthy if he could have his daughter. McCarthy said he was moving to Bismarck, where the girl could go to school. He had no other children, and he knew that Itatewin would hate to give the girl up, so he talked Ben out of the girl. He did bring the girl out and Ben held her in his arms for a while. He could see Itatewin through the window, and she recognized him. To avoid embarassment, he did not go in and Itatewin did not come out.

Ben Arnold continued freighting, packing, woodcutting, trailing cattle, and wolfing. He met most of the famous chiefs from the northern plains and the leading army officers. He even knew Calamity Jane, whom he described as a good teamster, herself.

Suggested reading: Lewis F. Crawford, *Rekindling Camp Fires* (Bismarck: Capital Book Co., 1926).

THE BUSINESS OF FREIGHTING

Richens Lacy Wooton was born in Mecklenburg County, Virginia, on May 6, 1816. When he was seven his father, a Virginia planter, moved to Christian County, Kentucky. Ten years later, tired of raising tobacco, 17-year-old Richens spent two years on a cotton plantation in Mississippi. Almost two years after that, eighteen and tired of farming in general, he went to Independence, Missouri, and got work as a teamster on a Bent & St. Vrain wagon train bound for Bent's Fort on the Arkansas River in present Colorado.

Thus Dick Wooton, as his new friends called him, began a career that would extend into trapping, building and operating a toll road, sheep herding (he trailed nine thousand head over sixteen hundred miles to Sacramento), guiding, scouting, and fighting Indians.

Wooton learned quickly as the seven-wagon train, each wagon pulled by ten or twelve mules, caught up with and joined a 57-wagon train bound for Santa Fe. Each night the wagons were parked in a circle, the men not on duty as guards sleeping inside the circle. The mules, themselves, were good guards. Their loud snorting often signaled that strangers were near.

The combined train was attacked by Comanches at the fork where the Pawnee empties into the Arkansas. In this unusual fight in bright moonlight the teamsters held off between 250 and 300 attackers, some armed with muskets but most with bows and arrows or spears. The Indians failed to run off the mule herd and retreated, leaving behind what Wooton called three "good" (dead) Indians.

Wooton behaved well in the fight. After his train reached Fort Bent he was put in charge of thirteen men and sent out on a trading expedition to Indians in what is now northern Colorado, Nebraska, and Wyoming.

Twenty years later Wooton was freighting between Fort Union in New Mexico Territory and Kansas City. His description of that operation is a fine account of long distance freighting.

They started from Fort Union on March 1, 1856. They had thirty six large freight wagons, each pulled by ten oxen. Wooton, the *major domo,* had two wagon-masters as assistants and two herders to drive the herd of forty animals, needed as replacements for those killed or injured, or, as often happened, who became sore-footed. They also had an ambulance for a sick teamster or occasional passengers. While he doesn't say, these were usually drawn by mules, and they certainly had riding mules with them.

The men were divided into four messes of ten men each. Each mess had its own cooking outfit. The men elected their cooks, who got extra pay and were relieved from guard duty.

The teamsters formed a "camp" corral at the end of each day by circling the wagons with the tongues turned outside, the left fore wheel up against the right rear wheel of the wagon in front. The oxen were unyoked, driven to water, and then watched as they grazed and slept.

Under attack they formed a fighting corral. This time the wagon tongues were inside the circle, the right front wheel up against the left rear wheel of the wagon in front. This put the oxen inside the circle where they were protected from being stampeded.

Each day's run started early in the morning when the oxen were driven into the circle and yoked up. The rearmost wagon each day moved to the front of the train the next.

They started out without breakfast, stopping about ten o'clock to eat. The oxen grazed with access to water until two or three. Then another run until evening brought them up to the daily average of fifteen to twenty miles. The round trip between Fort Union and Kansas City took four months.

Going east, the wagons were about half loaded. Wooton tried to buy or trade for enough furs that he could cover his expenses for the round trip. Each wagon carried from six to eight thousand pounds on the west bound trip. Sometimes they got as much as ten thousand pounds on a wagon. Two hundred thousand pounds was average for a thirty-six wagon train.

The freight charges at that time were eight dollars a hundred pounds, so the average gross was sixteen thousand dollars. Teamsters got twenty dollars a month, and the provisions cost about a thousand dollars for a round trip. The net profit for a trip was about ten thousand dollars, a "pretty good business," as Wooton admitted.

After the one trip to Kansas City in 1856, Wooton freighted military supplies from Fort Union to Albuquerque. His government contracts were as profitable as his freighting across the plains.

Freighting stopped in early winter. Then Wooton drove his oxen to the prairie country where they shifted for themselves until spring. He doesn't say anything about guarding the animals in winter or Indian losses during that season.

Suggested reading: Howard Louis Conard, *"Uncle Dick" Wooton* (Chicago: W. E. Dibble & Co., 1890).

BASQUE MULE PACKER

J ean Jaques Caux, a mule packer in British Columbia, was hard to understand. Born in the Basque region of southwestern France, his unique language mixed Basque, French, and Spanish, dressed up with words adopted from Mexicans, Germans, Scots, Irish, and Chinese. His helpers thought his proficiency in multi-lingual swearing made his mules the most urbane animals in the world. Everyone called him Cataline.

His favorite beverage was cognac, but Cataline always left a little in the glass to sprinkle on his thick, black hair. Rubbing it into his scalp to the words, "A little insida; a little outsida," did wonders for him. He had few gray hairs when he died nearly a hundred years old. He never said "she, they, his, hers, its, or theirs;" everything was "he." A favorite caution to a new man was, "Watcha da sterna da mule."

Cataline had no formal education, but he could handle a sixty-mule train with no need for packing slips or invoices. He could sign his name and had an indestructible memory. He knew exactly what each pack contained, who owned it, and where it was going. Totally honest, he thought all others were, too. At the beginning of each season he borrowed what he needed from a bank or the Hudson's Bay Company, and then told his customers to just pay their charges directly to his creditor. He probably lost some in the transactions, but not enough that he worried.

Cataline reached British Columbia in the 1860s, by way of Mexico and California. The terminology he used (he called his helpers stevedores and his assistant *segundo*) suggested that he had packed in those places. He operated from as far south as Yale on the Fraser River all the way north to the Yukon.   He drove the largest and most efficient pack train in Western Canada.

This Basque mule packer cut an impressive figure. Average in height, he had broad shoulders and a deep chest, tapering down to a slim waist and narrow hips. Throughout his packing career he wore leather riding boots, a broad-brimmed sombrero, a boiled shirt (one for each trip), heavy wool pants, and a ten-inch-wide elaborately-buckled leather belt. He always wore gauntleted buckskin gloves in mosquito season, but never wore socks, even in winter.

A legend grew up that Cataline was impervious to cold. The police officer in charge at Hazelton knew him well and said he was the toughest man — Indian or white — he had ever met. He saw Cataline once on the Babine trail, asleep on a canvas spread on the ground.

"It was a frosty night," the officer said. He was fully clothed but had no cover. A small fire he had started had gone out. I stood a few minutes,

JEAN JAQUES CAUX (CATALINE)

British Columbia Archives

watching his deep breathing. His hair, beard, and clothing were covered with heavy frost, and he was having a good night's sleep."

Sometimes Cataline carried his own goods for trading with the natives. For those trading sessions he would add to his apparel a stiff collar, yellow with age and smelling of mule sweat. He would exchange his broad trail sombrero for a narrow little French hat made of horsehair, and add a long morning coat, green with age. Then he would move his broad leather belt to the outside of the coat and cover that with a red woolen sash. Finally, the riding boots were replaced with fancy-beaded moccasins. Then Cataline would pass out a generous supply of enormous cigars, and the trading would begin.

Cataline had a deep compassion for the natives. The pomp and ceremony that he incorporated into the trading sessions did not affect his honesty, integrity, and burning desire to see that the Indians were fairly treated at all times.

Cataline hardly ever lost any freight. But one time, when he was using both horses and mules, a Chinese stevedore mistakenly loaded brown sugar on horses instead of mules. Cataline knew that horses would lie down in water with a pack on, something mules would never do. He had either forgotten to tell the Chinese, or the man had forgotten his instructions. The day was scorching and the horses lay down as they crossed a stream. When they finally came up on the far bank, streaming brown syrup from their packs, Cataline cursed in eight languages.

One time when Cataline was making a short run from the Hudson's Bay Store in Hazleton to Babine he had a farrier remove the shoes from a mule.

"You mean you want new shoes?" the farrier asked.

"No," replied Cataline. "Leave 'em off. Four case eggs go Babine. I put 'em in one pack on dat mule. He (it was a jenny) go out dere no shoe maybe ten mile — he feet get sore. He walk easy like zee cat. Not break one egg going down hill other side."

The eggs were delivered, unbroken.

Cataline had only one possession that he treasured, a Mexican throwing knife that he kept razor sharp. He kept it in his right boot by day and under his head at night. One time a group of toughs from "outside" had a few too many and began heckling him. Finally, he walked quietly to the far side of the room and carefully examined a small mark on the wall. Then he backed up fifteen feet, drew his knife from his boot, and threw it directly into the spot. He recovered the knife, spun around to the hecklers and said, "Sacreedam — dat all I tell you dis time!" The heckling stopped.

Position and status meant nothing to the old packer. He thought all persons were equal. During the gold rush of 1898 the Canadian

Government sent troops to the Yukon to help the Mounted Police keep order. Cataline was hired to pack their baggage from a river boat on Telegraph Creek over one hundred sixty rugged miles to Atlin and Teslin Lakes. The troops were commanded by a pompous and arrogant officer. According to his custom, Cataline called the officer "boy," which didn't help much. The enlisted men disliked the officer, and they enjoyed the friction which kept growing between the two men.

The officer insisted on having all the soldiers' activities heralded by bugle calls. Reveille, breakfast, loading the pack train, camping for the day, retiring at night — nothing could happen until the bugle sounded off. So much metallic blaring terrified the mules and infuriated Cataline. The officer, having lost the last argument about the mules' nap time, kept the bugle busy. Then, as they entered deep muskeg, the officer decided his soldiers should lead the mules. Cataline rebelled loudly, profanely, and in all his languages. His perfectly obedient mules needed no leaders. No one had ever led them!

Soon a mule, baffled at being led, lost its footing and went down in the muskeg. It lay there, its hooves flailing the air as it squealed for help. The officer rode up to take charge and only made matters worse. By now Cataline had quieted down and sat on his horse, taking it all in.

When the officer realized he could not solve the problem he said, "Please, Mr. Cataline, what ever shall we do now?"

After an ominous silence, Cataline bellowed in triumph: "Blowa da buga, blowa da buga!"

Cataline never lost his gift for the theatrical. On his last pack trip he drove 1380 pack mules and horses, the longest pack train ever known in the Cariboo.

The Basque packer's many years of travels and campsites had helped develop the far-flung outposts of British Columbia and the Yukon. He spent his last years on a friend's ranch near Hazelton. They never found his treasured knife among his few possessions. His friends were sure he had flung it into the raging Skeena River, assuring himself that it would not fall into less worthy hands than his.

He was buried at Hazelton. A stone cairn with an embedded mule shoe marks the place.

Suggested reading: Cecile Carroll, "Cataline," in *True West*, (April, 1993).

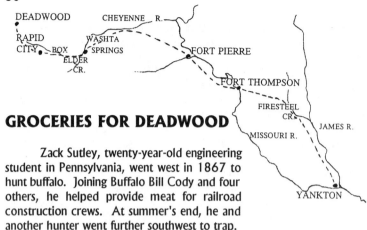

GROCERIES FOR DEADWOOD

Zack Sutley, twenty-year-old engineering student in Pennsylvania, went west in 1867 to hunt buffalo. Joining Buffalo Bill Cody and four others, he helped provide meat for railroad construction crews. At summer's end, he and another hunter went further southwest to trap.

For the next eight years, Sutley trapped, traveled, and guided others all over the west. He wintered once at Fort Churchill, on Hudson's Bay. After a short visit home, he returned west to become a freighter.

On December 15, 1877, Sutley led a ninety-six-yoke ox train out of Yankton, Dakota Territory, bound for Deadwood, four hundred forty miles away. He had twelve wagon loads of lumber going to Fort Pierre and eighteen wagon loads of flour, eggs, pork, butter and other provisions for Deadwood.

Swinging northwest between the Missouri and James Rivers, the train reached Firesteel Creek in five days. By Christmas they were back on the Missouri River at Fort Thompson.

The train crossed the Missouri River ice and reached Fort Pierre on New Year's Day. Sutley left the lumber at the fort, along with the wagons and bulls which had hauled it, plus four men to care for the animals. Although Sutley doesn't say so, one of the men left was probably George Flemming.

Flemming constantly had trouble yoking up. Oxen, like all draft animals, want the same partner and the same place in the team from one day to the next. Flemming seldom got it right.

"George," Sutley asked one day, "can't you tell these bulls apart."

"No sir, I never could tell one ox from another."

"Well, is there anything you can tell apart, one from another?"

"Yes sir, I can always tell sheep."

"How can you tell sheep apart?"

"By their faces — they all look different."

"I'll bet if we had sheep," another driver said amid the laughter, "it would be chickens you could tell apart."

The train continued west on January second. They reached the Cheyenne River, one hundred twenty miles away, in eight days. They had been traveling in deep snow and encountering bad storms ever since leaving Fort Thompson. On January 11, as they followed the Cheyenne River, they faced one of the worst blizzards Sutley had ever seen.

A northwest wind blew so hard the snow seemed to pummel them in sheets, rather than falling as flakes. A driver could see the wagon ahead only when the wind and blowing snow allowed ghostly outlines to appear briefly and then disappear. They barely kept the bulls on the trail.

They stopped in total darkness at five o'clock. They put the wagons in a circle, running log chains between to corral the bulls. The snow, soon drifted as high as the wagons, provided some relief from the wind.

The drivers normally slept in their wagons. On this night, they huddled by the stove in the cook tent. The bulls whistled as they breathed. Sutley worked among them all night, removing ice from their nostrils so they would not suffocate. The red-hot stove melted the snow which pressed against the tent. By morning the men were ankle-deep in cold mud.

They had been traveling with a man named Brown, who had seven yoke of oxen. Neither Brown nor his driver son would leave the tent during the night. Sutley had all he could do to keep his own bulls alive. Four of Brown's fourteen were dead by morning.

It took all the next day to shovel the wagons out and get the bulls on the prairie so they could paw through the snow for feed. They reached Washta Springs on the second day after the storm. Four men shoveled ahead of the wagons all that day.

The horse team with the tent and cook outfit reached the springs first. When the rest of the train pulled in, Sutley learned that an exhausted ox had been abandoned seven miles back. After he ate his supper, Sutley stuffed gunny sacks with hay and loaded them, plus two, two-gallon kegs of water across his saddle, and set out to find the ox. He drove the ox down a draw so it would have some protection from the wind, gave it a drink, and left the hay and the rest of the water. He got back to the train at midnight.

The next morning Sutley sent the train on ahead.

"I'll walk back, get the ox, and catch up by the time you reach Box Elder Creek," he said. "It's only ten miles. We'll camp there tonight. Be a short day."

The morning was mild, so he left his buffalo overcoat in the snow, along with his lunch and some hay for the ox, before starting back for the animal. He had no difficulty finding the ox and driving it up to the previous night's camp, where he fed it. He even spread his coat across the bull, as Sutley felt warm from the walking.

But snow began falling, and soon Sutley could no longer see the tracks of his train ahead. He was afraid to continue, thinking he might miss the train and the next campsite completely.

He found a draw where the snow was deep, and he dug a hole with his hands. He took his coat off the ox, leaving it to fend for itself. He put the coat on and crawled into the hole, carrying the stick he had used to drive the ox. Using the stick, he kept an air hole open into his frozen cave. Finally he could see stars and he knew it was no longer snowing.

Sutley was never worried about his safety, but he had never felt so alone in the universe.

"I felt very close to God," he wrote. "It was the longest night I ever spent. I crawled in at four in the afternoon, coming out at seven in the morning. I stayed awake the whole fifteen hours."

He found the ox a mile away in some willows. Two miles down the trail, he met two of his men coming back to look for him. They reached Rapid City the next day.

They stayed in Rapid City two weeks, making sleds to replace the wheels under the wagons. Sutley also sold some of his load, along with four yoke of oxen, so the train going on was smaller. The eight oxen brought a thousand dollars in gold. He traded the ox he had saved for hay to feed the other animals.

They got the wagon boxes on the sleds, loaded them up again, and pulled out for Deadwood. They spent all of the fourth day of that trip lowering the wagons into Deadwood Gulch. They had to rope each wagon to a tree, lower it as far as the rope reached, then tie another rope to a closer tree, and repeat that process until all the wagons had reached the bottom.

Deadwood was full of prospectors and animals. The weather had warmed, snow was melting, and the sleds sunk into the mud, halfway to the wagon boxes. How Sutley wished they had their wheels back!

Sutley's train was the only one to reach Deadwood that 1877-78 winter. He got unheard-of prices for his goods. Eggs sold for seventy-five cents a dozen, butter for a dollar a pound. Flour brought twenty-five dollars a hundred pounds, and pork brought that or better.

Sutley's oxen were in excellent condition. He had fed them hay from Yankton to Fort Pierre and grain from then on. He sold several oxen for beef. One bull brought one hundred seventy-five dollars. Calamity Jane said it was the finest ox she had ever seen.

Suggested reading: Zack T. Sutley, *The Last Frontier* (New York: The Macmillan Company, 1930).

THE BULLWHACKER

Nebraska State Historical Society

EARLY FREIGHTING TO DEADWOOD

Charles W. Allen was fifteen when his family gave up their Iowa farm and moved to Wamego in Pottawatomie County, Kansas. Charles got a job hauling lumber from Kansas River sawmills to the new town of Wichita being built one hundred fifty miles to the southwest.

He liked freighting. After an enlistment in the Kansas State Militia followed by a cattle drive to Wyoming and a ranch job near Fort Laramie, Charles hired on as a teamster with Cuny & Ecoffey Freighting in 1872. Most of their freighting was for the army.

The next year Charles married Emma Hawkins, 18-year-old niece of his boss, Adolph Cuny. Her mother was a mixed-blood Lakota woman. During a 52-year marriage that ended with Emma's death, she and Charles raised twelve children and had thousands of Indian friends.

Shortly before the marriage, Charles bought four horses and a wagon and started freighting on his own. He hauled hay and wood to Fort Laramie and Fort Fetterman and brought supplies up from the railroad in Cheyenne.

Charles was one of the first to haul into Deadwood after gold was discovered in the Black Hills. He made his first trip in 1876. Amos Bettelyoun with an eight-mule team and Austin Means with a team of six horses and mules traveled with Charles. They drove down to Cheyenne and had to wait a couple of days for their freight to arrive.

While waiting for the railroad train, they stayed in a collection of barns, corrals, and sleeping rooms, complete with iron cots and cooking utensils, at the northwest edge of town. They walked in to the bright lights area, where "joy was unconfined and pitfalls inseparable." Vaudeville and variety shows ran from three in the afternoon to three in the morning, with the Old McDaniels Theater the favorite. The theater had been built by James MacDaniels at the corner of Eddy Street and Sixteenth.

MacDaniels often ran the following ad in the *Cheyenne Leader:*

> 'Tis on the street that's yclept Eddy,
> Where Mac is always ever ready,
> To give bright hues to pale proboscis,
> And many gains, but never losses;
> Regale you with the best Havanas,
> Just fresh from Cuba's broad savannas –
> And mix up such a Thomas and Jerry,
> As would an Anchorite make merry.

The principal businesses were barber shops, followed by saloons, hotels, and eating places.

The many barber shops were supported by large numbers of freighters, cowboys, miners, and mountain men who arrived with dust-drenched whiskers and matted-down hair, looking for a haircut, shave, and bath. The barbers relied on shampoos for their big money. The freighters believed that some of the shops kept secret tins filled with lice taken from previous customers. If a customer declined to have a shampoo, the barber would step away for a moment. Shortly after returning, an adroit movement of the barber would produce a fat, lively grayback, apparently from the customer's head.

"Are you sure about that shampoo?" the barber would ask. "Look at what you've been totin' around."

Cheyenne was an all night town. There was never a time when all the saloons were closed.

The freight the three men picked up was what they called easy freight. It was easy to unload and load back if they got stuck, which often happened. Charles's load was sacked onions. They left Cheyenne in late June, and news of the Little Bighorn Battle arrived as they pulled out. They were not surprised when they reached Fort Laramie a few days later that the army held them up until enough wagons had gathered to travel safely through hostile Indian country.

During their five-day wait until thirty-six wagons had gathered and the army let them go, they heard about the massacre of the Metz family in Red Canyon, which they would be going through, and of other recent attacks. The army urged them to organize the train and to be constantly on the lookout.

They laid over a day at Running Water Creek to give everyone — especially the women in the families that were traveling — a chance to rest, bathe, and wash clothing. They also used the time to repair wagons and rearrange loads.

The next day after camping on Hat Creek they passed Warbonnet Creek, where Buffalo Bill, scouting for the 5 th Cavalry a few days before, had killed Cheyenne Chief Yellow Hair, collecting what Cody called the First Scalp for Custer.

Two days later they passed through Red Canyon and saw the place where the Metz family, with its several children, had been killed. The family had been traveling from Laramie City to Deadwood.

They laid over a day at Custer City to give everyone a chance to rest and clean up and to let the animals rest and graze. They had camped on questionable ground at Fort Laramie, and some had been infested with vermin. So, from early evening to the next forenoon the anthills around their camp were covered with soiled clothing. Employing ants to carry away the graybacks was often the first cycle in trailside laundry in the Old West.

Some of the men spent the afternoon scouting in the hills and they brought back many lustrous rubies (actually garnets). The pretty mineral specimens ranged in size from from a bead to a large garden pea.

That evening the relaxed travelers, probably remembering the first cycle of their earlier laundry, discussed the strength of an ant in proportion to its size. As the topic moved to other small animals, including lice, the discussion got heated. Finally one teamster offered to bet that a grayback could beat an ant in single bug to bug combat. Soon plugs of tobacco, boxes of matches, pen knives, and trinkets of all kinds were held by stakeholders as bets were made.

The fight promoter cleaned off a level spot and placed a perfectly clean plate on it. Then he carefully lowered the combatants into position in the middle of the plate while spectators cheered on their gladiator selections. The ant fell while trying to charge and grab the fat little louse. It crouched to charge again but slipped further back. Then it tried to slip in from the side or back of its adversary, but the grayback, slowly turning to meet every challenge, continued to occupy the center of the battleground. Finally, the ant fled to the plate's rim, but he was unable to climb over. Just then the herd was driven in, and the fight crowd left to feed their teams and do their evening chores. The ant backers lost their bets, but we don't know if one or both combatants survived.

Camping each night by clear, cool streams, they passed through Hill City and on to Deadwood, which they entered by going down a long, dangerous grade to the row of rough buildings at the bottom of the canyon. Before the grocer who received Charles's onions had finished measuring out the freighting charges in gold dust, his customers were lining up at the counter to pay twenty-five cents per pound for the onions.

Allen stayed three days in Deadwood before starting back to Fort Laramie. On the second night there, he and a couple of friends decided to take a stroll around and see the sights. Their evening of discovery was mostly just walking up one side of the street and back on the other, looking into each of the well-lighted places of amusement. However they did go into one and treat themselves to a beer and a cigar each.

Three years later Allen moved his family and freighting operations to the agency being built for the Oglala Lakota at Pine Ridge. In 1890 he was an eyewitness to the shootout at nearby Wounded Knee. By then Allen was a partner in a publishing venture and a special correspondent for the *New York Herald,* which published his account of the tragedy.

Suggested reading: Charles W. Allen, *From Fort Laramie to Wounded Knee* (Lincoln: University of Nebraska Press, 2001).

BLACK HILLS RENDEZVOUS

In early March, 1877, the Cheyenne and Black Hills Stage Company was loading up to nine stages a day for travel to Deadwood. Each Concord coach carried about eighteen passengers and sixteen hundred pounds of baggage. Cheyenne had become the rallying point for the Black Hills gold rush. The prospectors switching from the railroad to a stage at that point felt secure in travel, as no stage had yet been held up on that line.

The most popular driver on the line was twenty-six-year-old Johnny Slaughter, whose father, J. N. Slaughter, was the Cheyenne City Marshal. Johnny's mother was not in good health, so Johnny helped his father care for her when he was in town. The company had assigned Johnny to its mountain division because he was their best driver, fearless and dependable.

Although he probably didn't know it, Johnny had an interesting passenger on his stage when he left Cheyenne on March 20. A demure little black-eyed woman, Hattie Durbin was a direct descendant of John Alden, the first pilgrim to step on Plymouth Rock and the last surviving signer of the Mayflower Compact. Hattie's ancestor was Longfellow's main character in *The Courtship of Miles Standish*. She and her baby were joining her husband, Tom, who had been prospecting for a year. Tom's brother, John, traveled with her. Until the stage stopped for the first change of horses, Hattie thought her brother-in-law was going along to protect her, even though the stage held two other women traveling alone, one of them with a baby.

But at that stop, John handed her a package, saying, "This is some money. Put it in the bag with the baby's bottles. No one will suspect you of having it." She knew it was money and kept quiet, but she didn't know how much there was. The money Hattie hid with her baby's bottles was intended for the opening of a bank in Deadwood. If she had known it was ten thousand dollars in bills, she probably would have fainted.

Apparently the six robbers lying in wait had learned the currency was coming on the stage. After the holdup Tom told Hattie, "Oh, my God, Hattie! It's because of the money in this bag that Johnny Slaughter's body is waiting to be taken to Cheyenne."

This was apparently the gang's first attempt at robbery. Sam Bass, the leader, had grown up hating school but loving racehorses. After he moved from Indiana to Texas he tried freighting for the sheriff, but wanted his money to come easier, so he bought a two-year-old filly whose blood lines ran back to Steel Dust, the most famous thoroughbred in Texas before the Civil War. Then Bass went into partnership with Joel Collins, a Texas cowboy. They won a lot of money and horses with Collins persuading their victims that he knew all about Bass's horse and assuring them, "Your horse is bound to win."

When the law pressed too closely in Texas, they bought a trail herd of cattle with promissory notes, moved it to Nebraska and sold it, forgetting about the notes. Then they headed to the Black Hills gold rush in fall, 1876. The northern winter made prospecting too unpleasant for these men who preferred making money with their wits rather than their hands. They used the remainder of their proceeds from crime to buy a freighting outfit to operate between Deadwood and Cheyenne.

They lost sixty dollars on their first trip. "We better try the robbin' business," Bass told Collins.

They soon had a gang of six, adding Jim Berry, Frank Towle, Bill Reddy (sometimes called Reddy McKemma), and Bill Heffridge. The stage driven by Johnny Slaughter was to be their first project, as well as the first stage holdup in the Black Hills.. They moved two miles out of Deadwood to a place on Whitewood Creek, just above the mouth of Gold Run, and set up camp to wait for the stage. The March 25 night was cold, and they took along plenty of whiskey for warmth.

By the time Johnny Slaughter came around a rocky bend, the moonlight gleaming on his six white horses, the waiting robbers were all drunk.

"We'll stop 'em right here," said Bass, "and we won't kill nobody, neither. We don't need the law after us fer a mankillin'." He stepped out into the road, raised his pistol, and hollered, "Stop."

The stage driver was the idol of his day — like the matador or home run hitter or movie actor of other times. And Johnny Slaughter was the best and most popular driver in the Black Hills. He had proven his bravery in fights with Indians and his skill in maneuvering the stage over dangerous mountain roads. But there was no use arguing with an armed thug who had the drop on you. Johnny hollered, "Whoa," and pulled back on the reins.

But one of the horses shied at Reddy, weaving drunkenly and holding a shotgun. The gun fired, and the blast hit Johnny in the heart. Walter Iler, a passenger sitting next to Johnny with a few pellets of buckshot in his own arm, brought the horses to a halt. The robbers, frightened at the turn of events, fled, leaving Hattie Durbin undisturbed with her ten thousand dollars.

When the robbers reached Deadwood, Bass chased Reddy out of the gang and out of town for his carelessness in frightening the horses. Then Bass, Collins, Berry, and Heffridge followed. Frank Towle stayed in town and was arrested by Sheriff Seth Bullock. He was released when no passenger could identify him.

In the meantime, Walter Iler drove the stage on into Deadwood, arriving after midnight. Bullock led a posse back to the scene, but all they found was Johnny Slaughter's dead body.

They had a memorial service for Johnny at the Grand Central Hotel in Deadwood on the evening of March 27. A preacher officiated, and many women attended the service.

Marshal Slaughter arrived a few days later to claim his son's body and return it to Cheyenne for a second funeral on April 4. Over forty carriages followed the hearse as it was drawn slowly by six white stage horses. It was the longest procession ever seen in Cheyenne to that time. Johnny's mother died before the month was out, and she was buried beside her son.

The robber gang, less triggerman Reddy, stayed together until September, when they robbed a Union Pacific train in Big Springs, Nebraska. This time luck was with them and they got sixty thousand dollars. Then they split up.

Collins and Heffridge , leading an overburdened pack horse with their share of the railroad loot — gold coins from the San Francisco mint — ran into a posse in Kansas a month later. In a gun battle with a sheriff, a railroad detective, and ten cavalrymen from Fort Hays, they were both killed.

Berry was killed in Missouri shortly after. He had just changed several thousand dollars in gold coins for currency and an elegant suit of clothes.

Towne returned to the Black Hills and was killed in October during another stage holdup.

Bass got back to Texas where he gathered up a new gang and continued robbing stages and railroad trains. He died in a July, 1878, shootout while trying to rob a bank in Round Rock Texas.

When the Bass gang split up, Reddy went to Ohio. He got a life sentence for a later killing in that state.

The story of Bass's life became a legend in the west, sung around campfires and in bunkhouses by cowboys, miners, and drifters from Texas to Canada, from Kansas to California.

So on March 25, 1877, three trails crossed tragically near Deadwood, Dakota Territory. One was that of Sam Bass, celebrated in song and story. One was that of a descendant of a famous pilgrim — why don't you speak for yourself, John? And the trail ended that day for the most popular stage driver in the Black Hills.

Suggested reading: Agnes Wright Spring, *The Cheyenne and Black Hills Stage and Express Routes* (Lincoln: Univ. Of Neb. Press, 1948).

STANDOFF AT THE SPRING

Bill Hooker was seventeen in 1873 when he left his Wisconsin home for Cheyenne. His father had just lost a leg in a foundry accident, his mother had just died from tuberculosis, and Bill wanted to see the West. He had saved up eighty five dollars from his two years as a call boy on the Chicago and Northwestern Railroad. With the money in one pocket, a small derringer in the other, and a letter of introduction to the Union Pacific manager in Omaha, he headed west.

Bill announced in Omaha that he was already a railroad man, but if they didn't want to give him a pass to Cheyenne, he was willing to buy a full fare ticket.

"Railroad *man*," sputtered the ticket agent, looking at Bill who weighed all of a hundred pounds. "Maybe I'll give you a half-fare ticket."

"I don't want to seem impolite," Bill insisted, "but I ain't no half-fare fellow, you know."

Bill arrived in Cheyenne with no plans except to see life on the wild frontier. His eighty-five dollars was soon gone at the faro tables, and Bill became the newest bullwhacker on John Hunton's wagon train. They freighted north and northwest serving army posts.

Bill learned how to yoke and unyoke oxen, how to chain the teams to a freight wagon, how to crack the whip over his bulls, shouting gee, haw, and whoa when appropriate, and how to curse most of the time.

The crew made Bill the bread maker on the first trip, largely, he thought, because his hands were clean. They didn't stay clean long. His oxen pulled the mess wagon at the dusty, rear end of the train.

They played the usual jokes on Bill. But the common sense he had learned as a call-boy, waking grouchy engineers and conductors and staying at their front doors until he was sure they would report for duty, served him well. Soon, he was a popular member of the crew. Then the mess wagon and bread making duties were turned over to another new man.

Bill night-herded a while, and then got a splendid seven-yoke team to drive.

Much of the time Bill's train freighted army supplies from the Medicine Bow station on the Union Pacific to Fort Fetterman, a few days' travel to the north.

About 1875 Bill was working on the trail north from Cheyenne to the Red Cloud Agency in northwest Nebraska, near Fort Robinson. It was a hot afternoon, and Bill and another were stopped at a creek to fill the train's water kegs. After the train had pulled on ahead out of sight, a half dozen young Indians, none more than fourteen, suddenly appeared, all armed with bows and arrows.

Bill said he was plenty scared, but he knew the importance of acting calmly. He grabbed his rifle, but did not point it at anyone. They were hauling supplies to these Indians, but he knew the young men, away from the controlling influence of their tribe's warriors, would want to make a big show of their bravery and capture the supplies.

Bill smiled and acted as though he didn't understand when the first Indian pointed at the wagon. But when they swarmed into the wagon and tore open a sack of brown sugar, he raised his rifle and yelled at them.

Then one of the Indians fixed an arrow and bent his bow, the arrowhead pointing directly at Bill. Bill responded by pointing his rifle at the Indian, but the Indian just laughed.

The other Indians climbed down from the wagon and came forward quietly, obviously wondering what would happen next. At that point Bill's partner stepped forward, his rifle in his hands.

Bill then pointed his rifle at a nearby Indian, grabbed him by the elbow, pointed to the army canteen they had been using to fill the water kegs, and marched him to the creek. There Bill made it obvious what he expected the Indians to do.

When they had filled the kegs, Bill poured out a cup full of brown sugar, divided it among the Indians, and he and his partner strung out their bulls, marching the six would-be warriors to camp with them.

The wagon boss kept the young Indians with the train and fed them until they reached Fort Robinson. Then he turned them over to the agency authorities. He told Bill that if he hadn't shown his determination to not be bluffed, the Indians would have robbed them.

When Bill Hooker quit bullwhacking he worked on the Nash Ranch in the foothills of the Rockies in Wyoming. Mrs. Nash had known Bill's mother back in Wisconsin. Bill described hmself as wild and wooly and hard to curry when he showed up at the ranch. Mrs. Nash shouted. "Albert, Albert, come here quick. Here's Will Hooker." Then she turned to Bill. "Oh I'm glad your mother can't see you. You go right down to the creek and strip everything off, and I'll send you some of the boys' clothes."

Bill didn't know what she meant. He wore patched army pants, an army shirt, heavy cowhide boots, a belt of cartridges, a revolver, and a hat. And nothing else. No stockings, no underclothes, no coat, no vest. He thought it was a fair-weather rig for a real bullwhacker.

Suggested reading: William F. Hooker, *The Bullwhacker* (Yonkers: World Book Co., 1924).

NO INDIANS AROUND HERE

Sylvester Sherman grew up in Missouri, about forty-five miles north of Kansas City. In 1872 he went west to whack bulls for his brother, Rolon, who was hauling logs to a sawmill west of Denver. Two years later he went to Cheyenne to work for Heck Reel. Soon he was second boss under George Throstle.

In 1879, while Sherman was cowpunching with J. C. Shaw, he told Shaw about an Indian attack.

"It was early July in '76," Sylvester said as he and Shaw sat by their camp fire. "We was loading up government freight for Fort Fetterman. We had to hire all kinds of men from good bull whackers and Mexicans down to long haired Missourians. Heck Reel was there and he told Throstle to see each man had a forty-five sixshooter and a forty-four Winchester. He said they was to keep the rifles in the jocky boxes on the front ends of their wagons. There'd been plenty Indian sign on the North Platte that summer, and he wanted the rifles handy.

"We broke camp on the lake above Cheyenne on July seventh. We followed the old road toward the Black Hills until we got to Bordeaux. Then we took the cut-off past the Billy Bacon ranch on the Laramie, the old Tobe Miller ranch on Cottonwood Creek, and the St. Dennis ranch on Horseshoe until we struck the old road from Fort Laramie to Fort Fetterman. We camped at Elkhorn for the night.

"The next day as we started up the Elkhorn Hill, Throstle and I stayed back until the last wagon was up. After the wagons was all up, Throstle and I rode on ahead to look over the road. When we was about three hundred yards in front of the lead wagon, what seemed like a hundred Injuns jumped out of a draw and started shooting. Throstle got hit three times and me only once. Throstle threw up both his hands and shouted, "Oh, my God," and fell off his horse.

"The savages tried to cut me off from the train. I couldn't shoot as I was using both feet and both hands to pound my horse. As I got closer to the train the Injuns pulled away, but they hit Irish Peet in the leg. I heard Peet cussing and yelling, 'corral the wagons, Ves, or they'll kill ever one of us.'

"I hollered for the lead wagon to corral up. It didn't take long, but one wagon got left behind. Soon they was throwing off flour and using it to build a breastworks.

"The men were shooting their sixshooters. I hollered for the rifles, but only one man knew where they were. Instead of putting them in the jocky boxes like Heck Reel said, they had put them all in the bed of one wagon and piled five thousand pounds of flour on top.

"But we soon had that flour unloaded and the men all in place along the breastworks with their rifles. The Injuns thought we only had pistols, so they rode up close, screaming their hideous war whoops. They weren't hitting any of us, but they was doing plenty damage to the work cattle and the saddle horses. Then we opened up with our rifles and they fell back.

"We laid there all day, sort of a stand off on each side. When night come on the Injuns went up to the wagon that had been left behind. It was loaded with bacon and forty kegs of beer. They threw off the beer, rolling the kegs down a long hill. Then they set the bacon on fire. The blaze flamed up two hundred feet. We coulda seen to pick up a pin in the corral. We was sure our scalps were gone.

"But, for some reason, the Injuns didn't attack. Maybe they was busy with the beer. The next morning we drove our cattle back to Elkhorn for water. The man whose wagon was left behind had run to the corral without unhitching. We found the wheel team on the wagon had been burned to death and the next team scorched some. The front five teams had pulled loose and were grazing, still yoked together.

"We broke camp about eleven and stopped where Throstle had fallen. The savages had taken his clothes and scalped him and cut out his heart. We put him on a tarpaulin on top of the load and covered him up.

"As we went up the road we met two cowpunchers. We asked if they'd seen any Injuns. They laughed and said they didn't believe there was any in the country. They said they'd been on LaPrelle Creek for two years and hadn't see so much as a moccasin track.

"I told them we'd just had a fight yesterday. They laughed again and said, 'Show us the signs.' I handed one of them my bridle reins and stepped up on the brake. I pulled the tarp back so they could see Throstle's body. They dropped my reins, spun their horses around, and headed for Fort Fetterman like jockeys riding the last quarter of a mile race.

"We camped at La Bonte that night and got to Fetterman the next day, where we gave poor Throstle a decent burial.

Suggested reading: J. C. Shaw, "Indian Story of Sylvester Sherman" in *Annals of Wyoming v. 3, no. 3,* (January, 1926).

WYOMING BLIZZARD

Early February, 1883, was a bad time for the J. L. Sanderson & Company stage line, furnishing mail and passenger service from the Union Pacific Railroad at Green River, Wyoming, to Fort Washakie, 150 miles north. The stages traveled through the towns of South Pass, Atlantic City, and Lander, and stopped at the stations of Big Sandy, Little Sandy, Dry Sandy, and Pacific Springs, between Green River and South Pass.

December and January had been free of heavy storms. While the weather had been cold and disagreeable with light snowfalls, the company had not yet changed from spring wagons to sleighs when George Ryder drove the southbound stage out of South Pass for Big Sandy on January 31.

Ryder, a young Texan, had come north the previous summer, and he had no experience with Wyoming winters. He had two passengers — eighteen-year-old Maggie Sherlock from South Pass, headed for school in Salt Lake City, and W. J. Stuart, superintendent of the stage line.

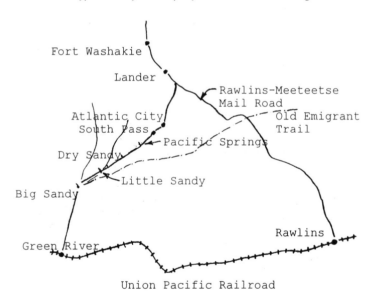

The morning of January 31 was dull and gloomy with snow falling out of an overcast sky. However there was no wind and the temperature was about normal. Ryder expected to make his run to Big Sandy without difficulty.

Heavy snow the day before had held up the southbound stage from Fort Washakie, but Stuart wanted to stake the road as far as Pacific Springs, so he loaded the stage with long willow poles and told Ryder to move out. He planted the poles every 25 to 30 feet so the drivers could find the road over the continental divide in case the snow got deep.

With the accumulating snow on the road and the stops for Stuart to set his stakes, they didn't reach Pacific Springs — twelve miles away — until noon. Stuart left the stage there to return on the northbound stage coming in from Big Sandy. Ryder changed horses, and he and his young passenger headed on for Dry Sandy, eleven miles away.

Ryder reached Dry Sandy without trouble, although travel was slow as the snow depth increased. Darkness was coming on when he reached the station. Even more ominous was the northeast wind that began drifting the snow. Ryder changed horses and headed out on the sixteen-mile run to Little Sandy.

Ryder became lost in the drifting, blinding snow. He returned to Dry Sandy, got his bearings, and set out again. Soon the young Texan was completely lost. He was so bewildered he did not know what course to pursue to go on his way or to return to the Dry Sandy Station, from which he had left twice already. Night had closed in, adding darkness to the blinding fury of the storm. The temperature had dropped rapidly and the cold was now intense. The howling wind had piled the snow into huge drifts which the horses floundered through with increasing difficulty. Finally, when his team, apparently down in some kind of low place out of the worst of the wind, refused to move, Ryder gave up and told Maggie they'd have to stay there until the storm was over.

Very likely Ryder had traveled in circles, as his stage was eventually found about a mile from the Dry Sandy Station. It was in a gulch that led directly to the station. Had he been more familiar with the country or able to see better, he might have been able to find his way back for the second time that day.

All night the blizzard raged in undiminished fury. Maggie Sherlock had warm clothes. Huddled in the box of the spring wagon, she protected herself from the wind and snow as well as she could. Ryder unhitched the horses and spent the night walking back and forth beside the wagon to keep up his circulation. Both hoped that with the light of day the storm would abate and they could reach shelter or be rescued.

But dawn on February 1 brought no let up in the fury of the blizzard.

Ryder made several futile tries during the day to get back to Dry Sandy. Each time he returned to report failure to his anxious passenger. He put Miss Sherlock on one of the horses, mounted the other and they tried to reach safety by horseback. This, too, failed and they returned to the stage, determined to remain until the storm had blown itself out.

When day broke on February 2, the cold was still intense, but the wind had slackened. Ryder, although badly frozen, made one more heroic effort to reach Dry Sandy Station. This time he succeeded, but he was so exhausted he could not return, and he was unable to give clear directions to stock tender John Thorn about where the stage was.

In a great stroke of luck, Thorn, after a long search, saw the seat of the spring wagon sticking up in the snow. He dug down and found Maggie, wrapped in a buffalo robe and barely alive. He got her back to the station where Mrs. Thorn cared for her until she was able to return to her home in South Pass.

The northbound stage to South Pass had left Big Sandy on the night of January 30. The driver was a man named Scott. He had one passenger, Bill Clark, a Lander Valley rancher. They reached Pacific Springs at noon the next day and picked up the superintendent, Stuart. Scott and Clark, exhausted from battling the blizzard all night, wanted to stay at the station. Stuart assured them they would have no trouble following the stakes he had just planted.

They struggled for eight miles, facing the biting wind and blinding snow. They had reached Fish Creek, only four miles from South Pass, but the horses refused to go any further, and night had come on. They turned the horses loose and started back on foot toward Pacific Springs. It was twice as far to shelter, but they would be going downhill with the wind, rather than against it. They traveled by leaving two men at each stake as they found it, while one man went forward until he found the next one. Yelling back and forth, they inched onward.

Stuart, wearing a heavy buffalo coat, could not keep up. He told the others to go on ahead. None of them reached Pacific Springs on that night.

On February 2 the blizzard subsided. Joe Johnson, the stock tender at Pacific Springs, started out for South Pass on foot. In three and a half miles he found the frozen, lifeless body of teamster Scott.

Loyal Manning, another stage employee at Pacific Springs, also set out, thinking he might find someone in distress. He saw something dark on a high ridge to the northwest. It turned out to be a large rock, swept clean by the wind, but in walking toward it, Manning came across what he thought might be a trail of someone on foot in the snow. He followed the faint markings as closely as he could, and after a mile he found Stuart. The man was lying in a deep gulch, almost buried in the snow, and barely conscious.

With great difficulty, Manning revived his superintendent, got him to his feet, and helped him to Pacific Springs Station. Stuart's feet, hands, and face were terribly frozen.

Clark's body was found several weeks later, barely a mile from Fish Creek, where they had abandoned the stage and started back on foot. Al Dougherty, a young and powerful man, was the driver on the south bound stage from Big Sandy to Green River. He waited all morning on January 31 for the stage from South Pass. Finally he pulled out without making the connection. Seven miles later, the blizzard was so fierce he could not go forward or back. He unhitched his horses and hung on to the traces as he drove them with the wind, hoping to find the Big Sandy River and follow it back to his station. He found the river, but the blizzard was so blinding and he was so bewildered he did not know which way to turn.

A low range of hills on the east side of the river provided some protection and a thicket of willows on the stream bank a little more. He thought about starting a fire, but realized in that hurricane of wind and the air filled with driving snow, he would never succeed. Instead he let one horse go and fastened the ends of the traces together on the other horse, looping them through the wide leather cartridge belt he was wearing. He spent that night, the next day, and all the next night driving the horse back and forth, as he stumbled along behind, trying to keep moving and alive. Many times he lost his grip and fell in the snow. But with a desperate tenacity he always got back to his feet, got his arms entwined into the tied-together traces and once more forced the horse slowly forward. He was only two hundred yards from the Big Sandy station when he fell down and was too exhausted to get back up or to force the horse on. In one last desperate effort he crawled on his hands and knees to the station.

Mr. and Mrs. Thorn did everything they could for George Ryder when he reached Dry Sandy, but he died three days later. Maggie Sherlock seemed to improve after she got home, but three weeks later she also succumbed.

Both Stuart and Dougherty survived. Stuart lost both hands, both ears, parts of both feet, and his nose. Dougherty lost one foot at the instep and the other above the ankle. He also lost most of his fingers.

With two teamsters dead and another permanently crippled, and with two passengers dead and their superintendent permanently crippled, the J. L. Sanderson & Company stage line was glad to see February, 1883, pass into history.

Suggested Reading: Tacetta B. Walker, *Stories of Early Days in Wyoming: Big Horn Basin* (Casper: Prairie Publishing Co., 1936).

BIG WAGONS AND MULES

W hen California-bound emigrants escaped from Death Valley in 1849, they said they had passed through the dregs of creation, a devilish wasteland of salt and saleratus. The first prospectors agreed — the place was a worthless sink of heat and alkali. But later prospectors discovered borax, not known during the gold rush to even be present in the United States.

The name for the mineral came from ancient Persia, and borax is now used in making hundreds of products, including glass, paint, fertilizer, detergents, and insulation, and in hundreds of chemical processes, including dyeing, printing, leather processing, photography, and softening water. But first if had to be hauled out of Death Valley, most appropriately named for its environment. (Interestingly, most present day borax mining is done in the nearby Mohave Desert, a more liveable place.)

By the late 1870s enough discoveries had been made that miners and refiners sought ways to haul the mineral 165 miles to the railroad at Mohave, California. This required the building of special wagons and the development of teamster techniques to traverse twisting, rocky trails during temperature extremes unknown elsewhere in this country. (They eventually realized it was impossible from the middle of June to the middle of September.)

William T. Coleman, purchaser of the original discovery claims of Aaron and Rosie Winters, told J. W. S. Perry what he wanted. Big freighters had come west on the Santa Fe Trail, and twenty-ox teams had hauled wagons into Virginia City, but Perry needed wagons to haul ten-ton payloads across the West's worst desert, making regular 330-mile round trips without breakdowns. They would have to be built, as none existed.

Perry built ten. Rear wheels were seven feet in diameter with eight-inch wide, half inch thick steel tires, shrunk on to wheels made from four-year-seasoned hickory. The forward wheels were five feet in diameter, similarly constructed. Axles were solid steel bars, three and a half inches square in the rear, slightly smaller in front. Wagon beds were sixteen feet long, four feet wide, and six feet deep. Each wagon weighed 7800 pounds and cost $900. In five years of constant use, there was not a single breakdown.

The skill of teamsters in training and driving mules matched that of the wagon builders. Two wagons were chained together, with a water wagon — usually 1200 gallons — pulled behind. Sometimes horses were used as wheelers, hitched directly to the wagon, as their weight — about 1800 pounds each — gave more control over the wagon tongue than mules

TWENTY-MULE TEAM BORAX WAGONS

Note the teamster riding the near mule, and the swamper in each wagon

could provide. Mules, weighing a thousand to 1300 pounds, would make up the other nine spans.

The span in front of the wheelers were the pointers. Then, continuing forward, came the sixes, eights, tens, twelves, fourteens, sixteens, eighteens, and leaders.

The team was controlled with a jerkline, commonly used in long freighting teams. The teamster rode the near wheeler, the left animal of the span next to the wagon. His one rein ran forward through harness rings from the near pointer to the near leader. It was loose from the pointer back to the teamster, so he had slack for making the whipping motions necessary to send signals the long distance. A steady pull told the near leader to turn left; a series of short jerks signaled a right turn.

Stage drivers, in contrast held as many reins as they had horses in their team. With a six-horse team, the driver would hold three reins in each hand, each rein connected to the bits in a span of horses. So a steady pull of the right hand would turn the heads of all six horses to the right, with the opposite result using the left hand. The stage driver could also rotate his fists so the pull was more on the leader span, less on the middle span, and least on the wheelers. The opportunity for graceful driving was present, and Hank Monk, famous driver from Carson City to Placerville, was considered the best. His horses didn't seem to be driven, they sailed.

A jockey stick connected the mules in a span, running from the hame (attached to the collar) of the near mule to the bit of its mate (the off mule). As each near mule made its turn it would pull or push its mate to follow.

The main pulling parts of a harness were the tugs which connected a mule's collar to the singletree behind its rear legs. The singletrees connected through an evener or spreader to a heavy chain running forward from the wagon. So when a span moved forward, each mule exerted an equal force (assuming no slacker) on the chain drawing the wagons. But turning corners required well-trained mules and help from the swamper, the teamster's assistant.

Suppose a right turn was required. The teamster, in coming in to the corner, would keep the mules as far left as he could, but eventually, as the mules turned to the right, the chain would be pulled closer to the inside of the curve. The pointers were trained to step over the chain when they saw the leaders begin the turn. Only one mule would step over, of course — the off mule for a right turn and the near one to turn left — so that the paired mules were both on the same side of the chain, the opposite side from the direction of the turn. Then they would "point" away from the chain, pulling it to one side so it would go around the curve the same as the mules did.

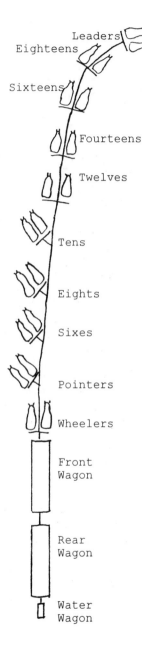

Leaders
Eighteens
Sixteens
Fourteens
Twelves
Tens
Eights
Sixes
Pointers
Wheelers
Front Wagon
Rear Wagon
Water Wagon

For sharp turns it was often necessary to have the sixes, eights, and sometimes even the tens step over the chain. Then the swamper would have to come forward and direct the required movements. The pointers, more used to the movement, would often respond to spoken commands — GEE for right and HAW for left — but the others would need help from the swamper. As the turn neared completion, the pointers would gradually come back next to the chain, where the one that had stepped over would have to step back to its regular place.

Most teamsters said the dumbest mule was smarter than the smartest horse. Among the mules, the near ones had to be smarter than the off ones, as they had to correctly respond to signals from the teamster or from watching the mule just ahead. The off mules were pushed or pulled into obedience. Of all the near mules, the leader had to be the smartest. While the others could mimic the ones ahead, SHE had to think for herself and do what the teamster wanted. Almost universally, that mule was a mare.

Tom Moore, a famous army teamster who served with General Crook in his campaigns, best reflected the widespread respect held for mules on the frontier. Moore said to Charles F. Lummis, who was gathering facts on life in the West, "Mules? Pardner, I want you to remember that God made mules a-purpose!" And, of course, Moore's boss was famous for, among other things, the fact that he always rode a mule.

Contrary to popular belief, most teamsters were quiet and patient with mules. The men who cursed until the air was blue were bullwhackers driving oxen. Sometimes you see drawings or read descriptions of teamsters using long whips on mules or horses. It didn't happen. No man could handle a whip that would reach out ninety feet.

Teamsters carried a short, flexible whip — usually wrapped around their neck — for gentle reminding on a mule having a bad day.

More likely a teamster would throw a small rock at a mule that needed a reminder. One Death Valley teamster said old man Moon could hit his eighteens from the jockey box on the wagon — about the same as a big league pitcher walking halfway back to second base and then turning to throw a strike.

Twenty-mule borax trains could travel fifteen miles a day loaded and twenty-two unloaded. They had one stretch of fifty miles without water, so they pulled a water wagon with them.

William T. Coleman, owner of the discovery mines who had the big wagons built in 1883, discovered still more borax. One rich ore was named colemanite in his honor. But he overextended himself, and his company failed in 1888. In 1893, J. W. S. Perry, who built the wagons, was superintendent of the Pacific Coast Borax Company, which by then included all of Coleman's properties. Coleman died that year, but not until he had paid off his creditors in full.

Two of the ten wagons were used to haul colemanite out of the Calico Mountains. Most of the others were apparently taken over by various freight and mining outfits. They show up in pictures from time to time.

Francis Marion "Borax" Smith, principal owner of the Pacific Coast Borax Company, had a giant steam tractor (Old Dinah) built to replace the mules in transporting borax. The tractor hauled heavy loads when it was working, but it would rear up on its hind wheels on steep grades, and it often dug itself down into soft roads until it was stuck. Many times teams of mules, driven by smiling teamsters, were used to pull Old Dinah out of self-excavated holes.

Suggested reading: Harold O Weight, *Twenty Mule Team Days in Death Valley* (Twenty Nine Palms: The Calico Press, 1955).

REWARD DENIED

Boone May, shotgun messenger for the Cheyenne and Black Hills Stage Line was a tough man. He was quick on the trigger and as much a killer as the outlaws he guarded the stage against. Men in his custody sometimes never reached the sheriff, but were shot while trying to escape.

May killed Frank Towle on September 13, 1878, while Towle was trying to hold up the stage at Old Woman's Fork. When the stage came in, May learned that a five thousand dollar reward had been offered for Towle — dead or alive — by the commissioners of Laramie County, Wyoming, for an earlier killing by Towle.

"You figger the reward's still good," May asked the station agent.

"It's a hundred fifty miles to Cheyenne," the agent replied. "That's a hell of a long way to haul a corpse for the reward."

"Don't need to haul it in," May replied. "The head oughta do."

So he returned to the place of the attempted holdup, cut off Towle's head, and wrapped it in a burlap sack. He took the next southbound stage with his grisly trophy. When the stage reached Cheyenne a few over-ripe days later, May shouldered the sack and carried it to the marshal's office.

"I bagged Frank Towle by myself, and I'm here for the reward," May stated as he rolled the head out on the marshal's desk.

"That reward was withdrawn a month ago," the flinty-eyed marshal said, apparently not shocked at all by the appearance of his desk. "And now you get this thing out of here. And you go get your burial permit and bury it proper, and you better have the five dollar fee ready, boy."

An often told story in Cheyenne was about the boys drowning out gophers who found a human head — not properly buried — north of town.

The stages went out of business when the smaller railroads were built. Boone May wrapped his six shooters and went to Bolivia. News came to Deadwood that he had shot an army officer in a quarrel over a woman and had gone to the hills to live with the Indians.

Years later, after most of his old cronies had died, a letter came saying Boone May was in Rio de Janeiro, waiting to follow a new gold rush to Brazil. "It's too bad," he wrote. "I think I got the yellow fever, and maybe I can't go."

Nothing more was ever heard. About a year before Seth Bullock died, he remarked that the fever probably murdered Boone May while he was trying to escape.

Suggested reading: Robert J. Casey, *The Black Hills and their Incredible Characters* (New York: Bobbs-Merrill Company, 1949).

ORDERING INFORMATION

True Tales of the Old West
is projected for 38 volumes.

For Titles in Print,
Ask at your bookstore
or write:

PIONEER PRESS
P. O. Box 216
Carson City, NV 89702-0216
Voice Phone (775) 888-9867
FAX (775) 888-0908

Other titles in progress include:

Frontier Artists	Ghosts & Mysteries
Army Women	Californios
Western Duelists	Doctors & Healers
Government Leaders	Homesteaders
Early Lumbermen	Old West Merchants
Frontier Militiamen	Scientists & Engineers
Frontier Teachers	Visitors to the Frontier